WORDSWORTH CLASSICS
OF WORLD LITERATURE

General Editor: Tom Griffith MA, MPhil

THE ART OF WAR
THE BOOK OF LORD SHANG

Sun Tzu

The Art of War

With a Commentary by General Tao Hanzhang
Translated by Yuan Shibing
Introduction by Robert Wilkinson

The Book of Lord Shang

Translated by J. J. L Duyvendak
Introduction by Robert Wilkinson

WORDSWORTH CLASSICS
OF WORLD LITERATURE

This edition published 1998 by Wordsworth Editions Limited
Cumberland House, Crib Street, Ware, Hertfordshire SG12 9ET

ISBN 1 85326 779 1

Typeset by Antony Gray
Printed and bound in Great Britain by
Mackays of Chatham, Chatham, Kent

CONTENTS OF THIS VOLUME

PREFATORY NOTE

Two systems for the romanisation of Chinese are currently in use in the western English-speaking world. One is of western origin – the Wade-Giles system – and the other, more recent and introduced by the Chinese themselves, called *pinyin*. Some translations of Chinese works use one system and some the other, making cross-reference occasionally confusing for non-specialists. To offset this difficulty, the following convention has been used in the introductions in this book: Chinese terms are given in their Wade-Giles version, but at their first occurrence the *pinyin* equivalent is given in square brackets immediately after the Wade-Giles version. For example, the name of the great Chinese historian of the first century BC is given as Ssu-ma Ch'ien [Sima Qian] and his work as *Shi Chi* [*Shiji*] (*Historical Records*). In about one third of cases, the two systems give the same romanisation. In these instances only one form appears at the first occurrence of the term concerned.

Most of the translator's extensive footnotes to *The Book of Lord Shang,* which deal almost exclusively with matters of textual corruption and variant readings, have been omitted. Scholars interested in these matters should consult the original edition of this work: London, Probsthain 1928.

THE ART OF WAR

THE ART OF WAR
CONTENTS

SUN TZU'S *THE ART OF WAR*

GENERAL TAO HANZHANG'S
COMMENTARY ON *THE ART OF WAR*

INTRODUCTION TO SUN TZU'S *THE ART OF WAR*

The two Chinese political classics in this book are the product of a time of intense turmoil in Chinese history. The first, Sun Tzu's *The Art of War* – the best-known of a considerable body of Chinese works on the subject – is concerned to analyse the nature of war and to show how victory can be assured; the second, *The Book of Lord Shang,* is a political treatise for the instruction of rulers. Its principal aim is to show how a strong state can be created and maintained, a state strong enough to resist its rivals and ultimately gain dominion over them. These texts are the exact reverse of ivory-tower speculations or armchair strategy: they are serious, urgent and practical responses to the desperate conditions prevailing at the time when they were written. They have both been immensely influential in China, and in the case of Sun Tzu in particular, outside it also. As so often, Chinese thought is shown by them to have its roots deep in reality in the widest sense of the term; and they are both – again not unusually for major Chinese works – characterised by a holistic response to the human predicament. Even amid the military recommendations of Sun Tzu and the political nostrums attributed to Lord Shang, Chinese spirituality in its Taoist form is never far distant. This same philosophy, which has as its goal a transforming personal encounter with ultimate reality, can and does inform every aspect of life, from the practices of the monk to the martial arts. We will return to this point, where appropriate, as we go along. To be unaware of it is to miss the deeper levels of meaning in these works.

As is often the case with the early masterpieces of Chinese thought, the date of composition and the authorship of Sun Tzu's *The Art of War (Sun-tzu ping fa* [*Sunzi bingfa*]) are not straightforward matters. There is a short biography of Sun Tzu in the greatest of early Chinese historical works, the *Historical Records* (Shi Chi [*Shiji*]) of Ssu-ma Ch'ien [Sima Qian] (1st century BC). Here Sun is described as a native of Ch'i [Qi] who secured service with Ho-lu [Helu], King of Wu, impressing the latter with his military skill. If this were accurate, it would follow that Sun lived around 500 BC, towards the end of the Spring and Autumn period (771–481 BC) in Chinese history. There is good reason to believe, however, that this date is incorrect (it has been the subject of scholarly dispute in China since at least the eleventh century AD). The reasons for this doubt are partly the absence of corroborative references to Sun in the appropriate major works of the Spring and Autumn period, and partly that the assumptions concerning war made in *The Art of War* do not reflect the conditions of the earlier time. Whoever wrote this text could assume the existence of large armies with professional officers, which would not have been the case during the Spring and Autumn period. At that time, war was a small-scale, amateurish, chaotic and brief form of self-indulgent adventuring on the part of rulers rather than the serious, professional business envisaged in this text. It is now thought likely that this text was composed during the Warring States period of Chinese history (403–221 BC). It bears the imprint of a single mind, and whoever its author was clearly had direct experience of war. I will continue to refer to the author as Sun Tzu, since this is both convenient and the usage sanctioned by tradition, but in the knowledge that the real authorship of the text is a mystery.

The Warring States period is aptly named. During the two and a quarter centuries of its duration, China as a unified state did not exist. By the end of the preceding Spring and Autumn period, itself marked by regular wars, what was finally to become China consisted of seven powerful and fifteen less powerful states. As its name suggests, the Warring States period was one in which the more powerful autonomous states vied with each other for dominance, swallowing up their smaller neighbours as necessary. The history of the period is accordingly one of constant warfare, alliance and counter-alliance, of treaties made and broken. Unsurprisingly, the nature of war itself changed as the period wore on. As it became clear that political stability could not be achieved easily, war ceased to be adventuring and became a desperately serious matter. The size of armies grew; campaigns became more protracted; the economic burden of maintaining the state in a condition to support an armed conflict became a subject of concern, and – again unsurprisingly – there emerged a class of professional officers who devoted their lives to the successful conduct of war. As the opening remark of *The Art of War* puts it – without exaggeration – war had become the most serious business of the state, the key to survival or ruin. It was a condition for survival that the state had an efficient army well commanded, and it is probable that the author of *The Art of War* was drawn from this class of professional fighters. In this text, he sums up the fruit of his experience, and in thirteen short chapters tells us how to win.

The first key to success is deceiving the enemy: 'All warfare is based on deception. Therefore, when capable of attacking, feign incapacity; when active in moving troops, feign inactivity.' (ch. 1; cf ch. 7) To prevent the enemy from fathoming one's intentions is of the first importance. Thus deceived, the enemy will not know whether or where to attack or defend and thus will have to prepare on all fronts (ch. 6) Such an enemy has his forces stretched, is consequently weak everywhere and will certainly be defeated.

If it is essential to keep all knowledge of one's own operations secret, it is equally vital to know as much as possible of the enemy's plans. Good intelligence is a second essential in war, and this lies behind Sun Tzu's view that an extensive spy network is not an optional extra but a basic necessity (ch. 13, *passim*). Wars are won as a result of good 'foreknowledge' (i.e. intelligence), and this 'cannot be elicited from spirits, nor from gods, nor by analogy with past events, nor by astrologic calculations. It must be obtained from men who know the enemy situation.' (ch. 13) The army relies on the information gathered by spies for its every move. There is no place, Sun Tzu argues, where espionage is not possible, and a large network of well-paid spies is a necessary and worthwhile investment for the state. As Sun Tzu stresses on more than one occasion, knowledge or intelligence is of vital importance in war: 'Know the enemy and know yourself; in a hundred battles you will never be defeated.' (ch. 3)

The figure responsible for strategy, and so for deceiving the enemy and evaluating the intelligence gathered by the spies, is the commander, and it is clear from Sun Tzu's description of the ideal commander that this officer must have a range of experience, knowledge and other attainments of a very high order. Firstly and most obviously, he must be a good soldier, someone experienced in campaigning and with a good knowledge of the principles of attack and defence described in the text: he must know how best to use each type of ground, how to manoeuvre, how best to combine his regular and special forces, and so on (cf especially chs 7–11). Secondly, however, the ideal general is described in language of a kind one would not find in a western text. For example, he must be 'serene and inscrutable' (ch. 11), capable of making 'unfathomable plans' (ibid). These are the terms often used to describe the person who has reached the spiritual goal of Taoism, namely enlightenment, and it is clear from other remarks in the text that Sun's ideal commander has achieved some such state: 'How subtle and insubstantial, that the expert leaves no trace. How divinely mysterious, that he is inaudible. Thus he is master of the enemy's fate.' (ch. 6) These at first sight puzzling remarks cease to be so when considered in the context of Taoist theory and practice. The Taoist sage (*sheng*) is one who is perfectly attuned to the ultimate reality which lies behind (so to speak) the everyday world with which we are familiar in daily experience. Such a one has ceased to have egoistic intentions or purposes in any sense analogous to that in which an unenlightened person does. Rather (s)he is perfectly and spontaneously in accord with the flow of reality itself. Having no intentions, the sage does not need to use reason to work out how to implement them, and such a one will certainly be unfathomable and inscrutable to the rest of us, i.e. the unenlightened. (For more detail on the principles of Taoism and the nature of the sage, see *Tao te ching* in the Suggestions for Further Reading). The presence of this spiritual dimension is one of the ways in which *The Art of War* differs markedly from the work in the western tradition with which it is regularly compared, *On War* (*Vom Kriege*, 1833) by Clausewitz. The latter, though comparable to Sun Tzu's work on a number of issues to be noted below, is entirely without this dimension. The reason for this difference is the absence of a close analogue to Taoism in western culture.

As has been said, the Taoist adept responds spontaneously and appropriately to whatever conditions obtain, and this is a further quality which the commander must possess. As Sun Tzu points out – and as Clausewitz was to point out again somewhat later – circumstances never repeat themselves exactly, and so the rules of strategy can never be set out in such detail that every situation is catered for in advance (cf ch. 1): 'Therefore, when a victory is won, one's tactics are not repeated. One should always respond to circumstances in an infinite variety of ways.' (ch. 6) Again, whoever is in accord with the Tao, the ultimate reality, benefits from the energy and direction of the whole order of things and is unstoppable, and so 'a skilled commander seeks victory from the situation and does not demand it from his subordinates'. (ch. 5) The 'situation' is a manifestation of the direction of the order of things, to which the Taoist adept responds with total mastery and absolute spontaneity: such a one has no need to rely on the plans or actions of subordinates. In summary, then, the ideal commander must have the qualities of a Taoist adept. Only such a one can respond appropriately to the unpredictable and infinitely variable situations which obtain in war. Because every war is different, no specific rules of strategy or tactics can be formulated such that following them will always produce victory. Only the flexible, adaptable and inventive will win.

Moreover, success in war does not depend on military action alone. One of the most striking features of *The Art of War* is Sun Tzu's clear awareness of the context, both psychological and material, of war. To go to war when there are insufficient funds in the treasury is a recipe for failure and for the ultimate destruction of the state. War causes inflation, and inflation exhausts the country waging the war. The economic costs of war constitute one of the reasons for Sun Tzu's repeated stress on the need to win quickly: 'A speedy victory is the main object in war . . . there has never been a protracted war which benefited a country.' (ch. 9: cf ch. 11) The second reason for speed is the need to maintain morale, both in the army and in the state at large, a point which once again Clausewitz was to repeat. Weary soldiers long for home and do not fight with the same zeal as fresh troops, and those involved in a long campaign will be aware of the hardships being caused to their families by the war economy (cf ch. 7).

If all these conditions are met – if the right man is in command, able to deceive the enemy as to his intentions while well supplied with intelligence from an extensive spy network, and so on – then the ultimate goal of war will be achieved. With regard to the nature of this final goal we come to one of the most marked of the contrasts between Sun Tzu and Clausewitz. For the latter, war is an act of force whose goal is to compel the enemy to do our will. The use of force is in theory (though, because of political constraints, not in practice) without limits. Clausewitz dismisses as dewy-eyed dreamers those who suggest that this can or ought to be done with little or no bloodshed. In war, he argues, one must not shrink from whatever bloodshed is necessary. Those who do shrink from it will be destroyed (cf Clausewitz, *On War* ch. 1). For Sun Tzu, the destruction implied in Clausewitz's remarks is to be avoided if at all possible, since the goal of war is *not* the wholesale destruction of the enemy: 'Generally, in war the best policy is to take a state intact; to ruin it is inferior to this. To capture the enemy's entire army is better than to destroy it.' (ch. 3) Behind this lies a further goal and ideal entirely absent from the western work, Sun Tzu's much quoted remark that 'To subdue the enemy without fighting is the supreme excellence.' (ch. 3) The least good way to subdue an enemy is military action: next best is to disrupt the enemy's alliances by strategy; best of all is to employ strategy to defeat the strategy of the enemy. The greatest commander is not the victor of a hundred battles but he who does not have to do battle at all to win. Only the Taoist adept will be able to achieve this ideal, which presupposes a level of penetrating insight not given to ordinary mortals. It would be foolish to suggest that the history of warfare in China shows that this ideal was realised. Like all ideals, it lies at the limits of the humanly achievable: what is of real interest is that it *is* the proposed ideal. At least Sun Tzu does propose an alternative to the appalling brutalities of actual war.

Such in brief outline are the leading ideas of this short but immensely influential text. As we shall see when we turn presently to General Tao Hanzhang's commentary on it, it has been revered in China for centuries, and its reputation and influence have survived the transformation of China into a Communist state. Again, it has been known and studied in Japan for centuries, certainly from the mid-eighth century AD and in all probability before that. It has also been fairly well known in the west for longer than is the case with many other Chinese classics. The first French translation appeared in 1772, to be followed by a Russian version in 1860, and by English and German versions in the twentieth century. The flow of English versions in particular has increased, and it is unlikely that this would occur unless Sun Tzu had something important to say. Indeed, it is one of the best-known texts on war in world literature, a testimony to the great penetration of its central ideas.

ROBERT WILKINSON
Department of Philosophy
The Open University

SUGGESTIONS FOR FURTHER READING

Other versions of The Art of War *with introductions offering different perspectives on the work*

T. Cleary (tr.), *The Art of War*, Shambhala, Boston and London 1988

S. B. Griffith (tr.), *The Art of War*, Oxford University Press 1963 and later editions

Other Chinese texts on war

R. D. Sawyer, (ed. and tr.): *The Art of the Warrior: Leadership and Strategy from the Chinese Military Classics*, Shambhala, Boston and London 1996

As noted above. Sun Tzu's *The Art of War* is the best known but by no means the only important Chinese military classic. This thematically arranged work is a good point at which to begin study of some of the other major works of this kind. Here extracts from Sun Tzu are amplified by extracts from seven other works.

Other works referred to

Karl von Clausewitz, *On War*, Wordsworth, Ware 1997

Lao Tzu, *Tao te ching*, Wordsworth, Ware 1997

Ssu-ma Ch'ien, *Records of the Grand Historian of China*, tr. Burton Watson, 2 vols, Columbia University Press, New York 1961

CHAPTER 1

Estimates

War is a matter of vital importance to the state; a matter of life or death, the road either to survival or to ruin. Hence, it is imperative that it be studied thoroughly.

Therefore, appraise it in terms of the five fundamental factors and make comparisons of the various conditions of the antagonistic sides in order to ascertain the results of a war. The first of these factors is politics; the second, weather; the third, terrain; the fourth, the commander; and the fifth, doctrine. Politics means the thing which causes the people to be in harmony with their ruler so that they will follow him in disregard of their lives and without fear of any danger. Weather signifies night and day, cold and heat, fine days and rain, and change of seasons. Terrain means distances, and refers to whether the ground is traversed with ease or difficulty and to whether it is open or constricted, and influences your chances of life or death. The commander stands for the general's qualities of wisdom, sincerity, benevolence, courage, and strictness. Doctrine is to be understood as the organisation of the army, the gradations of rank among the officers, the regulation of supply routes, and the provision of military materials to the army.

These five fundamental factors are familiar to every general. Those who master them win; those who do not are defeated. Therefore, in laying plans, compare the following seven elements, appraising them with the utmost care.

1 Which ruler is wise and more able?
2 Which commander is more talented?
3 Which army obtains the advantages of nature and the terrain?
4 In which army are regulations and instructions better carried out?
5 Which troops are stronger?
6 Which army has the better-trained officers and men?

7   Which army administers rewards and punishments in a
    more enlightened and correct way?

By means of these seven elements, I shall be able to forecast
which side will be victorious and which will be defeated.

The general who heeds my counsel is sure to win. Such a general
should be retained in command. One who ignores my counsel is
certain to be defeated. Such a one should be dismissed.

Having paid attention to my counsel and plans, the general must
create a situation which will contribute to their accomplishment.
By 'situation' I mean he should take the field situation into
consideration and act in accordance with what is advantageous.

All warfare is based on deception. Therefore, when capable of
attacking, feign incapacity; when active in moving troops, feign
inactivity. When near the enemy, make it seem that you are far
away; when far away, make it seem that you are near. Hold out
baits to lure the enemy. Strike the enemy when he is in disorder.
Prepare against the enemy when he is secure at all points. Avoid
the enemy for the time being when he is stronger. If your
opponent is of choleric temper, try to irritate him. If he is arrogant,
try to encourage his egotism. If the enemy troops are well prepared
after reorganisation, try to wear them down. If they are united, try
to sow dissension among them. Attack the enemy where he is
unprepared, and appear where you are not expected. These are the
keys to victory for a strategist. It is not possible to formulate them
in detail beforehand.

Now, if the estimates made before a battle indicate victory, it is
because careful calculations show that your conditions are more
favourable than those of your enemy; if they indicate defeat, it is
because careful calculations show that favourable conditions for a
battle are fewer. With more careful calculations, one can win; with
less, one cannot. How much less chance of victory has one who
makes no calculations at all! By this means, one can foresee the
outcome of a battle.

CHAPTER 2

Waging War

In operations of war – when one thousand fast four-horse chariots, one thousand heavy chariots, and one thousand mail-clad soldiers are required; when provisions are transported for a thousand *li*; when there are expenditures at home and at the front, and stipends for entertainment of envoys and advisers – the cost of materials such as glue and lacquer, and of chariots and armour, will amount to one thousand pieces of gold a day. One hundred thousand troops may be dispatched only when this money is in hand.

A speedy victory is the main object in war. If this is long in coming, weapons are blunted and morale depressed. If troops are attacking cities, their strength will be exhausted. When the army engages in protracted campaigns, the resources of the state will fall short. When your weapons are dulled and ardour dampened, your strength exhausted and treasure spent, the chieftains of the neighbouring states will take advantage of your crisis to act. In that case, no man, however wise, will be able to avert the disastrous consequences that ensue. Thus, while we have heard of stupid haste in war, we have not yet seen a clever operation that was prolonged. For there has never been a protracted war which benefited a country. Therefore, those unable to understand the evils inherent in employing troops are equally unable to understand the advantageous ways of doing so.

Those adept in waging war do not require a second levy of conscripts or more than two provisionings. They carry military equipment from the homeland, but rely on the enemy for provisions. Thus, the army is plentifully provided with food.

When a country is impoverished by military operations, it is due to distant transportation; carrying supplies for great distances renders the people destitute. Where troops are gathered, prices go up. When prices rise, the wealth of the people is drained away.

When wealth is drained away, the people will be afflicted with urgent and heavy exactions. With this loss of wealth and exhaustion of strength the households in the country will be extremely poor and seven-tenths of their wealth dissipated. As to government expenditures, those due to broken-down chariots, worn-out horses, armour and helmets, bows and arrows, spears and shields, protective mantlets, draft oxen, and wagons will amount to 60 percent of the total.

Hence, a wise general sees to it that his troops feed on the enemy, for one *zhong* of the enemy's provisions is equivalent to twenty of one's own and one *shi* of the enemy's fodder to twenty *shi* of one's own.

In order to make the soldiers courageous in overcoming the enemy, they must be roused to anger. In order to capture more booty from the enemy, soldiers must have their rewards.

Therefore, in chariot fighting when more than ten chariots are captured, reward those who take the first. Replace the enemy's flags and banners with your own, mix the captured chariots with yours, and mount them. Treat the prisoners of war well, and care for them. This is called 'winning a battle and becoming stronger'.

Hence, what is valued in war is victory, not prolonged operations. And the general who understands how to employ troops is the minister of the people's fate and arbiter of the nation's destiny.

CHAPTER 3

Offensive Strategy

Generally, in war the best policy is to take a state intact; to ruin it is inferior to this. To capture the enemy's entire army is better than to destroy it; to take intact a regiment, a company, or a squad is better than to destroy them. [Regiment, company, and squad are *lu*, *zu*, and *wu* in Chinese. In ancient China, five hundred soldiers made up a *lu*, one hundred a *zu*, and five a *wu*.] For to win one hundred victories in one hundred battles is not the acme of skill. To subdue the enemy without fighting is the supreme excellence.

Thus, what is of supreme importance in war is to attack the enemy's strategy. Next best is to disrupt his alliances by diplomacy. The next best is to attack his army. And the worst policy is to attack cities. Attack cities only when there is no alternative because to prepare big shields and wagons and make ready the necessary arms and equipment require at least three months, and to pile up earthen ramps against the walls requires an additional three months. The general, unable to control his impatience, will order his troops to swarm up the wall like ants, with the result that one-third of them will be killed without taking the city. Such is the calamity of attacking cities.

Thus, those skilled in war subdue the enemy's army without battle. They capture the enemy's cities without assaulting them and overthrow his state without protracted operations. Their aim is to take all under heaven intact by strategic considerations. Thus, their troops are not worn out and their gains will be complete. This is the art of offensive strategy.

Consequently, the art of using troops is this: When ten to the enemy's one, surround him. When five times his strength, attack him. If double his strength, divide him. If equally matched, you may engage him with some good plan. If weaker numerically, be capable of withdrawing. And if in all respects unequal, be capable of eluding him, for a small force is but booty for one more powerful if it fights recklessly.

Now, the general is the assistant to the sovereign of the state. If this assistance is all-embracing, the state will surely be strong; if defective, the state will certainly be weak.

Now, there are three ways in which a sovereign can bring misfortune upon his army:

1 When ignorant that the army should not advance, to order an advance; or when ignorant that it should not retire, to order a retirement. This is described as 'hobbling the army'.

2 When ignorant of military affairs, to interfere in their administration. This causes the officers to be perplexed.

3 When ignorant of command problems, to interfere with the direction of fighting. This engenders doubts in the minds of the officers.

If the army is confused and suspicious, neighbouring rulers will take advantage of this and cause trouble. This is what is meant by: 'A confused army leads to another's victory'.

Thus, there are five points in which victory may be predicted:

1 He who knows when he can fight and when he cannot will be victorious.

2 He who understands how to fight in accordance with the strength of antagonistic forces will be victorious.

3 He whose ranks are united in purpose will be victorious.

4 He who is well prepared and lies in wait for an enemy who is not well prepared will be victorious.

5 He whose generals are able and not interfered with by the sovereign will be victorious.

It is in these five matters that the way to victory is known. Therefore, I say: Know the enemy and know yourself; in a hundred battles, you will never be defeated. When you are ignorant of the enemy but know yourself, your chances of winning or losing are equal. If ignorant both of your enemy and of yourself, you are sure to be defeated in every battle.

CHAPTER 4

Dispositions

The skilful warriors in ancient times first made themselves invincible and then awaited the enemy's moment of vulnerability. Invincibility depends on oneself, but the enemy's vulnerability on himself. It follows that those skilled in war can make themselves invincible but cannot cause an enemy to be certainly vulnerable. Therefore, it can be said that, one may know how to win, but cannot necessarily do so.

Defend yourself when you cannot defeat the enemy, and attack the enemy when you can. One defends when his strength is inadequate; he attacks when it is abundant. Those who are skilled in defence hide themselves as under the ninefold earth; [in ancient China, the number nine was used to signify the highest number.] Those in attack flash forth as from above the ninefold heavens. Thus, they are capable both of protecting themselves and of gaining a complete victory.

To foresee a victory which the ordinary man can foresee is not the acme of excellence. Neither is it if you triumph in battle and are universally acclaimed 'expert', for to lift an autumn down requires no great strength, to distinguish between the sun and moon is no test of vision, to hear the thunderclap is no indication of acute hearing. In ancient times, those called skilled in war conquered an enemy easily conquered. And, therefore, the victories won by a master of war gain him neither reputation for wisdom nor merit for courage. For he wins his victories without erring. Without erring he establishes the certainty of his victory; he conquers an enemy already defeated. Therefore, the skilful commander takes up a position in which he cannot be defeated and misses no opportunity to overcome his enemy. Thus, a victorious army always seeks battle after his plans indicate that victory is possible under them, whereas an army destined to defeat fights in the hope of winning but without any planning. Those skilled in war cultivate their policies and strictly adhere to the laws and regulations. Thus, it is in their power to control success.

Now, the elements of the art of war are first, the measurement of space; second, the estimation of quantities; third, calculations; fourth, comparisons; and fifth, chances of victory. Measurements of space are derived from the ground. Quantities derive from measurement, figures from quantities, comparisons from figures, and victory from comparisons. Thus, a victorious army is as one *yi* [an ancient Chinese weight, approximately equivalent to 24 ounces] balanced against a grain, and a defeated army is as a grain balanced against one *yi*.

It is because of disposition that a victorious general is able to make his soldiers fight with the effect of pent-up waters which, suddenly released, plunge into a bottomless abyss.

CHAPTER 5

Posture of Army

Generally management of a large force is the same as management of a few men. It is a matter of organisation. And to direct a large force is the same as to direct a few men. This is a matter of formations and signals. That the army is certain to sustain the enemy's attack without suffering defeat is due to operations of the extraordinary and the normal forces. Troops thrown against the enemy as a grindstone against eggs is an example of a solid acting upon a void.

Generally, in battle, use the normal force to engage and use the extraordinary to win. Now, the resources of those skilled in the use of extraordinary forces are all infinite as the heavens and earth, as inexhaustible as the flow of the great rivers, for they end and recommence – cyclical, as are the movements of the sun and moon. They die away and are reborn – recurrent, as are the passing seasons. The musical notes are only five in number, but their combination gives rise to so numerous melodies that one cannot hear them all. The primary colours are only five in number, but their combinations are so infinite that one cannot visualise them all. The flavours are only five in number, but their blends are so various that one cannot taste them all. In battle, there are only the normal and extraordinary forces, but their combinations are limitless; none can comprehend them all. For these two forces are mutually reproductive. It is like moving in an endless circle. Who can exhaust the possibility of their combination?

When torrential water tosses boulders, it is because of its momentum; when the strike of a hawk breaks the body of its prey, it is because of timing. Thus, the momentum of one skilled in war is overwhelming, and his attack precisely timed. His potential is that of a fully drawn crossbow; his timing, that of the release of the trigger.

In the tumult and uproar, the battle seems chaotic, but there must be no disorder in one's own troops. The battlefield may seem in confusion and chaos, but one's array must be in good order. That will be proof against defeat. Apparent confusion is a product of good order; apparent cowardice, of courage; apparent weakness, of strength. Order or disorder depends on organisation and direction; courage or cowardice on circumstances; strength or weakness on tactical dispositions. Thus, one who is skilled at making the enemy move does so by creating a situation, according to which the enemy will act. He entices the enemy with something he is certain to want. He keeps the enemy on the move by holding out bait and then attacks him with picked troops.

Therefore, a skilled commander seeks victory from the situation and does not demand it of his subordinates. He selects suitable men and exploits the situation. He who utilises the situation uses his men in fighting as one rolls logs or stones. Now, the nature of logs and stones is that on stable ground they are static; on a slope, they move. If square, they stop; if round, they roll. Thus, the energy of troops skilfully commanded in battle may be compared to the momentum of round boulders which roll down from a mountain thousands of feet in height.

CHAPTER 6

Void and Actuality

Generally he who occupies the field of battle first and awaits his enemy is at ease, and he who comes later to the scene and rushes into the fight is weary. And, therefore, those skilled in war bring the enemy to the field of battle and are not brought there by him. One able to make the enemy come of his own accord does so by offering him some advantage. And one able to stop him from coming does so by preventing him. Thus, when the enemy is at ease be able to tire him, when well fed to starve him, when at rest to make him move.

Appear at places which he is unable to rescue; move swiftly in a direction where you are least expected.

That you may march a thousand *li* without tiring yourself is because you travel where there is no enemy. To be certain to take what you attack is to attack a place the enemy does not or cannot protect. To be certain to hold what you defend is to defend a place the enemy dares not or is not able to attack. Therefore, against those skilled in attack, the enemy does not know where to defend, and against the experts in defence, the enemy does not know where to attack.

How subtle and insubstantial, that the expert leaves no trace. How divinely mysterious, that he is inaudible. Thus, he is master of his enemy's fate. His offensive will be irresistible if he makes for his enemy's weak positions; he cannot be overtaken when he withdraws if he moves swiftly. When I wish to give battle, my enemy, even though protected by high walls and deep moats, cannot help but engage me, for I attack a position he must relieve. When I wish to avoid battle, I may defend myself simply by drawing a line on the ground; the enemy will be unable to attack me because I divert him from going where he wishes.

If I am able to determine the enemy's dispositions while, at the same time, I conceal my own, then I can concentrate my forces and his must be divided. And if I concentrate while he divides, I can use my entire strength to attack a fraction of his. Therefore, I will be numerically superior. Then, if I am able to use many to strike few at the selected point, those I deal with will fall into hopeless straits. The enemy must not know where I intend to give battle. For if he does not know where I intend to give battle, he must prepare in a great many places. And when he prepares in a great many places, those I have to fight will be few. For if he prepares to the front, his rear will be weak, and if to the rear, his front will be fragile. If he strengthens his left, his right will be vulnerable, and if his right, there will be few troops on his left. And when he sends troops everywhere, he will be weak everywhere. Numerical weakness comes from having to guard against possible attacks; numerical strength from forcing the enemy to make these preparations against us.

If one knows where and when a battle will be fought, his troops can march a thousand *li* and meet on the field. But if one knows neither the battleground nor the day of battle, the left will be unable to aid the right and the right will be unable to aid the left, and the van will be unable to support the rear and the rear, the van. How much more is this so when separated by several tens of *li* or, indeed, by even a few! Although I estimate the troops of Yüe as many, of what benefit is this superiority with respect to the outcome of war? Thus, I say that victory can be achieved. For even if the enemy is numerically stronger, I can prevent him from engaging.

Therefore, analyse the enemy's plans so that you will know his shortcomings as well as strong points. Agitate him in order to ascertain the pattern of his movement. Lure him out to reveal his dispositions and ascertain his position. Launch a probing attack in order to learn where his strength is abundant and where deficient. The ultimate in disposing one's troops is to conceal them without ascertainable shape. Then the most penetrating spies cannot pry nor can the wise lay plans against you. It is according to the situations that plans are laid for victory, but the multitude does not comprehend this. Although everyone can see the outward aspects, none understands how the victory is achieved. Therefore, when a victory is won, one's tactics are not repeated. One should always respond to circumstances in an infinite variety of ways.

Now, an army may be likened to water, for just as flowing water avoids the heights and hastens to the lowlands, so an army should avoid strength and strike weakness. And as water shapes its flow in accordance with the ground, so an army manages its victory in accordance with the situation of the enemy. And as water has no constant form, there are in warfare no constant conditions. Thus, one able to win the victory by modifying his tactics in accordance with the enemy situation may be said to be divine. Of the five elements [water, fire, metal, wood and earth], none is always predominant; of the four seasons, none lasts forever; of the days, some are long and some short, and the moon waxes and wanes. That is also the law of employing troops.

CHAPTER 7

Manoeuvring

Normally, in war, the general receives his commands from the sovereign. During the process from assembling the troops and mobilising the people to blending the army into a harmonious entity and encamping it, nothing is more difficult than the art of manoeuvring for advantageous positions. What is difficult about it is to make the devious route the most direct and to turn disadvantage to advantage. Thus, march by an indirect route and divert the enemy by enticing him with a bait. So doing, you may set out after he does and arrive at the battlefield before him. One able to do this shows the knowledge of the artifice of diversion.

Therefore, both advantage and danger are inherent in manoeuvring for an advantageous position. One who sets the entire army in motion with impediments to pursue an advantageous position will not attain it. If he abandons the camp and all the impediments to contend for advantage the stores will be lost. Thus, if one orders his men to make forced marches without armour, stopping neither day nor night, covering double the usual distance at a stretch, and doing a hundred *li* to wrest an advantage, it is probable that the commanders will be captured. The stronger men will arrive first and the feeble ones will struggle along behind; so, if this method is used, only one-tenth of the army will reach its destination. In a forced march of fifty *li*, the commander of the van will probably fall, but half the army will arrive. In a forced march of thirty *li*, just two-thirds will arrive. It follows that an army which lacks heavy equipment, fodder, food and stores will be lost.

One who is not acquainted with the designs of his neighbours should not enter into alliances with them. Those who do not know the conditions of mountains and forests, hazardous defiles, marshes and swamps, cannot conduct the march of an army. Those who do not use local guides are unable to obtain the advantages of the ground. Now, war is based on deception. Move when it is advantageous and create changes in the situation by dispersal and concentration of forces. When campaigning, be swift as the wind; in leisurely marching, majestic as the forest; in raiding and plundering, be fierce as fire; in standing, firm as the mountains. When hiding, be as unfathomable as things behind the clouds; when moving, fall like a thunderbolt. When you plunder the countryside, divide your forces. When you conquer territory, defend strategic points. Weigh the situation before you move. He who knows the artifice of diversion will be victorious. Such is the art of manoeuvring.

The Book of Military Administration says: 'As the voice cannot be heard in battle, drums and gongs are used. As troops cannot see each other clearly in battle, flags and banners are used.' Now, gongs and drums, banners and flags are used to unify the action of the troops. When the troops can be thus united, the brave cannot advance alone, nor can the cowardly withdraw. This is the art of directing large masses of troops. In night fighting, use many torches and drums, in day fighting, many banners and flags, in order to guide the sight and hearing of our troops.

Now, an army may be robbed of its spirit and its commander deprived of his confidence. At the beginning of a campaign, the spirits of soldiers are keen; after a certain period time, they flag, and in the later stage thoughts turn towards home. And therefore, those skilled in war avoid the enemy when his spirit is keen and attack him when it is sluggish and his soldiers homesick. This is control of the moral factor. In good order, they await a disorderly enemy; in serenity, a clamorous one. This is control of the mental factor. Close to the field of battle, they await an enemy coming from afar; at rest, they await an exhausted enemy; with well-fed troops, they await hungry ones. This is control of the physical factor. They do not engage an enemy advancing with well-ordered banners nor one whose formations are in impressive array. This is control of the factor of changing circumstances.

Therefore, the art of employing troops is that when the enemy occupies high ground, do not confront him uphill, and when his back is resting on hills, do not make a frontal attack. When he pretends to flee, do not pursue. Do not attack troops whose spirits are keen. Do not swallow bait. Do not thwart an enemy who is returning homewards.

Leave a way of escape to a surrounded enemy, and do not press a desperate enemy too hard. Such is the art of employing troops,

CHAPTER 8

The Nine Variables

In general, the system of employing troops is that the commander receives his mandate from the sovereign to mobilise the people and assemble the army.

You should not encamp on grounds hard to approach. Unite with your allies on grounds intersected with highways. Do not linger on desolate ground. In enclosed ground, resort to stratagem. In death ground, fight a last-ditch battle.

There are some roads which must not be followed, some troops which must not be attacked, some cities which must not be assaulted, and some ground which should not be contested. There are also occasions when the commands of the sovereign need not be obeyed. Therefore, a general thoroughly versed in the advantages of the nine variable factors knows how to employ troops. One who does not understand their advantages will not be able to use the terrain to his advantage even though he is well acquainted with it. In the direction of military operations, one who does not understand the tactics suitable to the nine variable situations will be unable to use his troops effectively, even if he understands the 'five advantages' [referring to the five situations mentioned at the beginning of this paragraph].

And for this reason, a wise general in his deliberations must consider both favourable and unfavourable factors. By taking into account the favourable factors, he makes his plan feasible; by taking into account the unfavourable, he may avoid possible disasters.

He who wants to subdue dukes in neighbouring states does so by inflicting injury upon them. He who wants to control them does so by keeping them constantly occupied, and he who makes them rush about does so by offering them ostensible advantages.

It is a doctrine of war not to assume the enemy will not come but rather to rely on one's readiness to meet him, and not to presume that he will not attack but rather to make oneself invincible.

There are five qualities which are fatal in the character of a general: if reckless, he can be killed; if cowardly, captured; if quick-tempered, he can be provoked to rage and make a fool of himself; if he has too delicate a sense of honour, he can be easily insulted; if he is of a compassionate nature, you can harass him.

Now these five traits of character are serious faults in a general and in military operations are calamitous. The ruin of the army and the death of the general are inevitable results of these shortcomings. They must be deeply pondered.

CHAPTER 9

On the March

When an army takes up a position and confronts the enemy, it has to observe and judge the enemy situation. In doing so, it should pay attention to the following:

When crossing the mountains, be sure to stay close to valleys; when encamping, select high ground facing the sunny side; when high ground is occupied by the enemy, do not ascend to attack. So much for taking a position in mountains.

After crossing a river, you must move some distance away from it. When an advancing enemy crosses water, do not meet him in midstream. It is advantageous to allow half his force to cross and then strike. If you wish to give battle, do not confront your enemy near the water. Take a position on high ground facing the sun. Do not take a position at the lower reaches of the enemy. This relates to positions near a river.

Cross salt marshes speedily. Do not linger in them. If you encounter the enemy in the middle of a salt marsh, you must take a position close to grass and water with trees to your rear. This has to do with taking up a position in salt marshes.

On level ground, occupy a position which facilitates your action. With heights to your rear and right, the field of battle is to the front and the rear is safe. This is how to take up a position on level ground.

Generally, these are advantageous principles for encamping in the four situations named. By using them, the Yellow Emperor conquered his four neighbouring sovereigns. [Legend has it that the Yellow Emperor was the most ancient emperor in China; he reigned about five thousand years ago.]

In battle, all armies prefer high ground to low, and sunny places to shady. If an army occupies high ground, which is convenient for living, it will not suffer from countless diseases, and this will spell victory. When you come to hills, dikes, or embankments, you must take a position on the sunny side. These are all advantageous methods, gained from the help the ground affords. When rain falls in the upper reaches of a river and foaming water descends, those who wish to ford must wait until the waters subside. Where there are precipitous torrents such as 'heavenly wells', 'heavenly prisons', 'heavenly nets', 'heavenly traps' and 'heavenly cracks' – you must march speedily away from them. Do not approach them. Keep a distance from them and draw the enemy towards them. Face them and cause the enemy to put his back to them. When, on the flanks of the army, there are dangerous defiles or ponds covered with aquatic grasses where reeds and rushes grow, or forested mountains with dense tangled undergrowth, you must carefully search them out, for these are places where ambushes are laid and spies are hidden.

When the enemy is nearby but remains calm, he is depending on a favourable position. When he challenges battle from afar, he wishes to lure you to advance; when he is on easy ground, he must be in an advantageous position. When the trees are seen to move, it means the enemy is advancing. When many screens have been placed in the undergrowth, it is for the purpose of deception. Birds rising in flight are a sign that the enemy is lying in ambush; when the wild animals are startled and flee, the enemy is trying to take you unawares.

Dust spurting upwards in high straight columns indicates the approach of chariots. When it hangs low and is widespread, it betokens that infantry is approaching. When dust rises in scattered areas, the enemy is collecting and bringing in firewood; when there are numerous small patches which seem to come and go, he is encamping the army. When the enemy's envoys speak in humble terms, but the army continues preparations, that means it will advance. When their language is strong and the enemy pretentiously advances, these may be signs that the enemy will retreat. When light chariots first go out and take position on the flanks, the enemy is forming. When without a previous understanding the enemy asks for a truce, he must be plotting. When his troops march speedily and he parades his battle chariots, he is expecting to rendezvous with reinforcements. When half his force advances and half withdraws, he is attempting to decoy you. When his troops lean on their weapons, they are famished. When drawers of water drink before carrying it to camp, his troops are suffering from thirst. When the enemy sees an advantage but does not advance to seize it, he is fatigued. When birds gather above the enemies camp sites, they are unoccupied. When at night the enemy's camp is clamorous, it betokens nervousness.

When his troops are disorderly, the general has no prestige. When his flags and banners are shifted about constantly, he is in disarray. If the officers are short-tempered, they are exhausted. When the enemy feeds grain to the horses and kills its cattle for food, and when his troops neither hang up their cooking pots nor return to their shelters, the enemy is desperate. When the troops continually gather in small groups and whisper together, the general has lost the confidence of the army. Too frequent rewards indicate that the general is at the end of his resources; too frequent punishments that he is in acute distress. If the officers at first treat the men violently and later are fearful of them, it shows supreme lack of intelligence. When the enemy's troops march up angrily and, although facing you, neither join battle for a long time nor leave, the situation requires great vigilance and thorough investigation.

In war, numbers alone confer no advantage. It is sufficient if you do not advance relying on sheer military power. If you estimate the enemy situation correctly and then concentrate your strength to overcome the enemy, there is no more to it than this. He who lacks foresight and underestimates his enemy will surely be captured by him.

If troops are punished before their loyalty is secured, they will be disobedient. If not obedient, it is difficult to employ them. If troops have become attached to you, but discipline cannot be enforced, you cannot employ them. Thus, command them with civility but keep them under control by iron discipline, and it may be said that victory is certain. If orders are consistently carried out to instruct the troops, they will be obedient. If orders are not consistently carried out to instruct them, they will be disobedient.

If orders are consistently trustworthy and carried out, it shows that the relationship of a commander with his troops is satisfactory.

CHAPTER 10

Terrain

Ground may be classified according to its nature as accessible, entangling, temporising, precipitous, distant, or having narrow passes. Ground which both we and the enemy can traverse with equal ease is called accessible. On such ground, he who first takes high sunny positions, and keeps his supply routes unimpeded, can fight advantageously. Ground easy to reach but difficult to get out of is called entangling. The nature of this ground is such that if the enemy is unprepared and you sally out, you may defeat him. If the enemy is prepared and you sally out, but do not win, and it is difficult for you to return, it is unprofitable. Ground equally disadvantageous for both the enemy and ourselves to enter is called temporising. The nature of this ground is such that although the enemy holds out a bait, I do not go forth but entice him by marching off. When I have drawn out half his force, I can strike him advantageously. If I first occupy narrow passes, I must block the passes and await the enemy. If the enemy first occupies such ground and blocks the defiles, I should not attack him; if he does not block them completely, I may do so. On precipitous ground, I must take a position on the sunny heights and await the enemy. If he first occupies such ground, I march off; I do not attack him. When at a distance from an enemy of equal strength, it is difficult to provoke battle and unprofitable to engage him.

These are the principles relating to six different types of ground. It is the highest responsibility of the general to inquire into them with the utmost care.

There are six conditions in which troops fail. These are: flight, insubordination, collapse in disorder, distress, disorganisation, and rout. None of these disasters can be attributed to natural causes, but to the fault of the general.

Other conditions being equal, if a force attacks one ten times its size, the result is flight. When soldiers are strong and officers weak, the army is insubordinate. When the officers are valiant and the soldiers ineffective, the result is collapse. When officers are angry and insubordinate, and on encountering the enemy rush into battle with no understanding of the feasibility of engaging and without awaiting orders from the commander, the army is in distress. When the general is morally weak and without authority, when his instructions and guidance are not enlightened, when there are no consistent rules to guide the officers and men, and when the formations are slovenly, the result is disorganisation. When a commander unable to estimate his enemy uses a small force to engage a large one, or weak troops to strike the strong, or when he fails to select shock troops for the van, the result is rout. When any of these six conditions prevails, the army is on the road to defeat. It is the highest responsibility of the general that he examine them carefully.

Conformation of the ground is of the greatest assistance in battle. Therefore, virtues of a superior general are to estimate the enemy situation, and to calculate distances and the degree of difficulty of the terrain so as to control victory. He who fights with full knowledge of these factors is certain to win; he who does not will surely be defeated. If the situation is one of victory, but the sovereign has issued orders not to engage, the general may decide to fight. If the situation is such that he cannot win, but the sovereign has issued orders to engage, he need not do so. And therefore, the general who in advancing does not seek personal fame, and in retreating is not concerned with disgrace, but whose only purpose is to protect the country and promote the best interests of his sovereign, is the precious jewel of the state.

A general regards his men as infants who will march with him into the deepest valleys. He treats them as his own beloved sons and they will stand by him unto death. If a general indulges his men but is unable to employ them, if he loves them but cannot enforce his commands, if the men are disorderly and he is unable to control them, they may be compared to spoiled children, and are useless.

If I know that my troops are capable of striking the enemy, but do not know that he is invulnerable to attack, my chance of victory is but half. If I know that the enemy is vulnerable to attack, but do not know that my troops are incapable of striking him, my chance of victory is but half. If I know that the enemy can be attacked and that my troops are capable of attacking him, but do not realize that the conformation of the ground makes fighting impracticable, my chance of victory is but half. Therefore, when those experienced in war move, they are never bewildered; when they act, their resources are limitless. And therefore, I say: Know the enemy, know yourself; your victory will never be endangered. Know the ground, know the weather; your victory will then be complete.

CHAPTER 11

The Nine Varieties of Ground

In respect to the employment of troops, ground may be classified as dispersive, frontier, key, open, focal, serious, difficult, encircled, and desperate.

When a feudal lord fights in his own territory, he is in dispersive ground. When he makes but a shallow penetration into enemy territory, he is in frontier ground. Ground equally advantageous to occupy is key ground. Ground equally accessible is open. When a state is enclosed by three other states, its territory is focal. He who first gets control of it will gain the support of the majority of neighbouring states. When the army has penetrated deep into hostile territory, leaving far behind many enemy cities and towns, it is in serious ground. When the army traverses mountains, forests, or precipitous country, or marches through defiles, marshlands or swamps, or any place where the going is hard, it is in difficult ground. Ground to which access is constricted, where the way out is tortuous, and where a small enemy force can strike a larger one, is called encircled. Ground in which the army survives only if it fights with the courage of desperation is called desperate. And therefore, do not fight in dispersive ground; do not stop in the frontier borderlands.

Do not attack an enemy who occupies key ground first; in open ground, do not allow your formations to become separated and your communications to be blocked. In focal ground, ally with neighbouring states; in serious ground, gather in plunder. In difficult ground, press on; in encircled ground, devise stratagems; in desperate ground, fight courageously.

In ancient times, those described as skilled in war made it impossible for the enemy to unite his front and his rear, for his divisions both large and small to cooperate, for his good troops to succour the poor, and for officers and men to support each other.

When the enemy's forces were dispersed, they prevented him from assembling them; even when assembled, they threw him into disorder. They concentrated and moved when it was advantageous to do so; when not advantageous, they halted. Should one ask: 'How do I cope with a well-ordered enemy host about to attack me?' I reply: 'Seize something he cherishes and he will conform to your desires.' Speed is the essence of war. Take advantage of the enemy's unpreparedness, make your way by unexpected routes, and attack him where he has taken no precautions.

The general principles applicable to an invading force are that when you have penetrated deeply into hostile territory your army is united and the defender cannot overcome you. Plunder fertile country to supply your army with plentiful provisions. Pay heed to nourishing the troops; do not unnecessarily fatigue them. Unite them in spirit; conserve their strength. Make unfathomable plans for the movements of the army. Throw the troops into a position from which there is no escape, and even when faced with death they will not flee. For if prepared to die, what can they not achieve? Then officers and men together put forth their utmost efforts. In a desperate situation, they fear nothing; when there is no way out, they stand firm. Deep in a hostile land they are bound together, and there, where there is no alternative, they will engage the enemy in hand-to-hand combat. Thus, such troops need no encouragement to be vigilant. Without extorting their support, the general obtains it; without inviting their affection, he gains it; without demanding their discipline, he wins it. Prohibit superstitious doubts and do away with rumours; then nobody will flee even facing death. My officers have no surplus of wealth, but it is not because they disdain riches; they have no expectation of long life, but it is not because they dislike longevity. On the day the army is ordered to set out, the tears of those seated soak their garments – the tears of those reclining course down their cheeks. But throw them into a situation where there is no escape and they will display the immortal courage of Zhuan Zhu and Cao Kuei. [Zhuan Zhu and Cao Kuei both lived in the Spring and Autumn Period, and were said to be brave warriors undaunted in the face of death.]

Now, the troops of those adept in war are used like the 'simultaneously responding snake' of Mount Ch'ang. When struck on the head, its tail attacks; when struck on tail, its head attacks;

when struck in the centre, both head and tail attack. Should one ask: 'Can troops be made capable of such instantaneous coordination?' I reply. 'They can.' For, although the men of Wu and Yüeh hate one another, if together in a boat tossed by the wind they would cooperate as the right hand does with the left. Thus, in order to prevent soldiers from fleeing, it is not sufficient to rely upon hobbled horses or buried chariot wheels. To achieve a uniform level of valour relies on a good military administration. And it is by proper use of the ground that both strong and weak forces are used to the best advantage. Thus, a skilful general conducts his army just as if he were leading a single man, willy-nilly, by the hand.

It is the business of a general to be serene and inscrutable, impartial and self-controlled. He should be capable of keeping his officers and men in ignorance of his plans. He changes his methods and alters his plans so that people have no knowledge of what he aims at. He alters his camp sites and marches by devious routes, and thus makes it impossible for others to anticipate his purpose. The business of a general is to kick away the ladder behind soldiers when they have climbed up a height. He leads the army deep into hostile territory and there releases the trigger. He burns his boats and smashes his cooking pots; he drives his men now in one direction, then in another, like a shepherd driving a flock of sheep, and no one knows where he is going. To assemble the army and throw it into a desperate position is the business of the general. To take different measures suited to the nine varieties of ground, to take aggressive or defensive tactics in accordance with different situations, and to understand soldiers' psychological states under different circumstances, are matters that must be studied carefully by a general.

Generally, when invading hostile territory, the deeper one penetrates, the more cohesion it brings; penetrating only a short way causes dispersion. Therefore, in dispersive ground, I would unify the determination of the army. In frontier ground, I would keep my forces closely linked. In key ground, I would hasten into the enemy's rear. In open ground, I would pay strict attention to my defences. In focal ground, I would consolidate my alliances. In serious ground, I would ensure a continuous flow of provisions. In difficult ground, I would march past the roads speedily. In encircled ground, I would block the points of access and egress. In desperate ground, I would make it evident that there is no chance of survival. For it is the nature of soldiers to resist when surrounded, to fight to the death when there is no alternative, and when desperate to follow commands implicitly.

One ignorant of the plans of neighbouring states cannot make alliances with them; if ignorant of the conditions of mountains, forests, dangerous defiles, swamps and marshes, he cannot conduct the march of an army; if he fails to make use of native guides, he cannot gain the advantages of the ground. A general ignorant of even one of these nine varieties of ground is unfit to command the armies of a hegemonic king. Now, when a hegemonic king attacks a powerful state, he makes it impossible for the enemy to concentrate his troops. He overawes the enemy and prevents his allies from joining him.

It follows that there is no need to contend against powerful combinations, nor is there any need to foster the power of other states. He relies for the attainment of his aims on his ability to overawe his opponents. And so he can take the enemy's cities and overthrow the enemy's state. Bestow rewards without respect to customary practice; publish orders without respect to precedent. Thus, you may employ the entire army as you would one man. Set the troops to their tasks without imparting your designs; use them to gain advantage without revealing the dangers involved. Throw them into a perilous situation and they will survive; put them in desperate ground and they will live. For when the army is placed in such a situation, it can snatch victory from defeat. Now, the crux of military operations lies in the pretence of following the designs of the enemy; and once there is a loophole that can be used, concentrate your forces against the enemy. Thus, even marching from a distance of a thousand *li*, you can kill his general. This is called the ability to achieve one's aim in an artful and ingenious manner.

Therefore, when the time comes to execute the plan to attack, you should close the passes, rescind the passports, have no further intercourse with the enemy's envoys, and exhort the temple council to execute the plans. When the enemy presents an opportunity, speedily take advantage of it. Seize the place which the enemy values without making an appointment for battle with him.

In executing the plan, you should change according to the enemy situation in order to win victory. Therefore, at first you should pretend to be as shy as a maiden. When the enemy gives you an opening, be swift as a hare and he will be unable to withstand you.

CHAPTER 12

Attack By Fire

There are five ways of attacking with fire. The first is to burn soldiers; the second, to burn provisions; the third, to burn equipment; the fourth, to burn arsenals; and the fifth, to burn the lines of transportation. To use fire, some medium must be relied upon. Equipment for setting fires must always be at hand. There are suitable times and appropriate days on which to raise fires. 'Times' means when the weather is scorching hot; 'days' means when the moon is in Sagittarius, Alpharatz, *I*, or *Zhen* constellations, for these are days of rising winds.

Now, in fire attacks, one must respond to the changing situation. When fire breaks out in the enemy's camp, immediately co-ordinate your action from without. But if the enemy troops remain calm, bide your time and do not attack at once. When the fire reaches its height, follow up if you can. If you cannot do so, wait. If you can raise fires outside the enemy camp, it is not necessary to wait until they are started inside. Set fires at suitable times. When fires are raised upwind, do not attack from downwind. When the wind blows during the day, it will die down at night. Now, the army must know the five different fire attack situations and wait for appropriate times.

Those who use fire to assist their attacks can achieve good results; those who use inundations produce a powerful effect. Water can isolate an enemy, but cannot destroy his supplies or equipment as fire can.

Now, to win battles and take your objectives but to fail to consolidate these achievements is ominous and may be described as a waste of time. And therefore, it is said that enlightened rulers must deliberate upon the plans to go to battle, and good generals carefully execute them. If not in the interests of the state, do not act. If you cannot succeed, do not use troops. If you are not in danger, do not fight a war. A sovereign cannot launch a war because he is enraged, nor can a general fight a war because he is resentful. For while an angered man may again be happy, and a resentful man again be pleased, a state that has perished cannot be restored, nor can the dead be brought back to life. Therefore, the enlightened ruler is prudent and the good general is warned against rash action. Thus the state is kept secure and the army preserved.

CHAPTER 13

Use of Spies

Now, when an army of one hundred thousand is raised and dispatched on a distant campaign, the expenses borne by the people together with disbursements of the treasury will amount to a thousand pieces of gold daily. In addition, there will be continuous commotion both at home and abroad, people will be exhausted by the corvée of transport, and the farm work of seven hundred thousand households will be disrupted. [In ancient times, eight families comprised a community. When one family sent a man to the army, the remaining seven contributed to its support. Thus, when an army of one hundred thousand was raised, those unable to attend fully to their own ploughing and sowing amounted to seven hundred thousand households.]

Hostile armies confront each other for years in order to struggle for victory in a decisive battle; yet if one who begrudges rank, honours and a few hundred pieces of gold remains ignorant of his enemy's situation, he is completely unaware of the interest of the state and the people. Such a man is no general, no good assistant to his sovereign, and such a sovereign no master of victory. Now, the reason a brilliant sovereign and a wise general conquer the enemy whenever they move, and their achievements surpass those of ordinary men, is their foreknowledge of the enemy situation. This 'foreknowledge' cannot be elicited from spirits, nor from gods, nor by analogy with past events, nor by astrologic calculations. It must be obtained from men who know the enemy situation.

Now, there are five sorts of spies. These are native spies, internal spies, double spies, doomed spies, and surviving spies. When all these five types of spies are at work and their operations are clandestine, it is called the 'divine manipulation of threads' and is the treasure of a sovereign. Native spies are those from the enemy's country people whom we employ. Internal spies are enemy officials whom we employ. Double spies are enemy spies whom we employ. Doomed spies are those of our own spies who are deliberately given false information and told to report it to the enemy. Surviving spies are those who return from the enemy camp to report information.

Of all those in the army close to the commander, none is more intimate than the spies; of all rewards, none more liberal than those given to spies; of all matters, none is more confidential than those relating to spy operations. He who is not sage and wise, humane and just, cannot use spies. And he who is not delicate and subtle cannot get the truth out of them.

Delicate, indeed! Truly delicate! There is no place where espionage is not possible. If plans relating to spy operations are prematurely divulged, the agent and all those to whom he spoke of them should be put to death.

Generally, in the case of armies you wish to strike, cities you wish to attack, and people you wish to assassinate, it is necessary to find out the names of the garrison commander, the aides-de-camp, the ushers, gatekeepers and bodyguards. You must instruct your spies to ascertain these matters in minute detail. It is essential to seek out enemy spies who have come to conduct espionage against you and to bribe them to serve you. Give them instructions and care for them. Thus, double spies are recruited and used. It is by means of the double spies that native and internal spies can be recruited and employed. And it is by this means that the doomed spies, armed with false information, can be sent to convey it to the enemy. It is by this means also that surviving spies can come back and give information as scheduled.

The sovereign must have full knowledge of the activities of the five sorts of spies. And the key is the skill to use the double spies. Therefore, it is mandatory that they be treated with the utmost liberality.

In old times, the rise of the Shang Dynasty was due to Yi Zhi, who had served under the Xia likewise, and the rise of the Zhou Dynasty was due to Lu Ya, who had served under the Yin. And therefore, only the enlightened sovereign and the wise general who are able to use the most intelligent people as spies can achieve great results. Spy operations are essential in war; upon them the army relies to make its every move.

INTRODUCTION TO
GENERAL TAO HANZHANG'S COMMENTARY

Almost from the time of its composition right up to the present day, Sun Tzu's *The Art of War* has been the subject of commentary by other Chinese writers. Many of these writers were also soldiers, and some were important figures in Chinese history in their own right, the most distinguished of all being the Han soldier and minister Ts'ao Ts'ao [Cao Cao] (155–200 AD). [On the major commentaries on Sun Tzu from earlier periods of Chinese history, see the works by Cleary, 1988 and 1989 in the Suggestions for Further Reading, below.] There are two principal reasons why so many commentaries on this short text should have been written.

The first derives from a pervasive feature of Chinese intellectual life, namely a reverence for tradition [on this cf e.g. Ames, 1994]. It follows from this fundamental principle that what is valued in intellectual production as elsewhere is continuity rather than innovation. Accordingly, thinkers who wish to set out new ideas do not present themselves as wishing to overthrow the valued masters. They find it far easier to gain a hearing by presenting ideas in the form of a commentary on those masters. This is a distinctly un-western approach. In the west, an individual gains *kudos* largely through ostentatious novelty, through being prominently the initiator of something new and different. A Chinese thinker would be far more likely to be accepted if viewed as someone who respects and continues a valued tradition.

The second reason for the proliferation of commentaries on Sun Tzu is specific to the text itself. As we have seen, Sun Tzu lays stress on the point that circumstances do not repeat themselves; tactics that win one battle are very unlikely to succeed a second time. The ideal commander, accordingly, is the one who responds fastest and most inventively to the conditions of the day. From this in turn it follows that no specific and exhaustive rules of war can be drawn up, and this is a major reason why Sun Tzu's own text is so brief. Beyond the very general recommendations he makes, there is nothing else that can usefully be said. With this idea the commentators tend to agree, but they point out that even if no rules for war can be formulated, Sun Tzu's text does benefit from historical illustration, from examples of wars won or lost as a result of following his advice or ignoring it. Accordingly, the commentaries are packed with examples drawn from Chinese history of incidents confirmatory of Sun's doctrines.

The respect the Chinese have for Sun Tzu's work, manifested in this centuries-long tradition of commentary, did not terminate with the communist revolution. Mao Tse-tung [Mao Zedong] admired *The Art of War,* and it is still read and used as a military textbook. The commentary on Sun Tzu which is printed here is by an officer in the People's Liberation Army (PLA), General Tao Han-chang [Tao Hanzhang] (b.1917) – not only an experienced field commander but also a writer and lecturer on military affairs. General Tao, as might be expected, writes about Sun Tzu not only in the light of his own experience of war and his knowledge of Chinese military history, but also from the standpoint of a man who wholeheartedly accepts the Maoist version of the Marxist philosophy of dialectical materialism. Much of his terminology, and his interpretation and final judgment of Sun Tzu, follow from the Maoist beliefs he takes for granted. While this is not the place for a full exposition of Maoism, it is as well to have an outline idea of what this philosophy is before reading the general's text.

The basic assertions of this philosophy are: (a) that the whole of reality [i.e. all there is] is material in nature; none of it is mental or spiritual; and (b) that the material which makes up all there is is in a state of constant change. Further, this change follows a universal pattern or is of a universal type which is labelled *dialectical.* Behind this notion of dialectical change lies the intuition that reality is never stable: the nature of things is always characterised by a certain inherent or inner tension which forever seeks to resolve itself, and it is the working out of this ceaseless tension which manifests itself as change in the universe. Marxists put this point by asserting that at any given time, reality can be said to be characterised by *contradiction*, a term which General Tao uses frequently. In Maoist Marxism in particular, this term 'contradiction' is used in a very extended sense. It is not used in the strictly logical sense in which two incompatible statements are said to contradict each other, e.g. 'unicorns exist' contradicts 'unicorns do not exist'. In Mao's sense of the term, contradiction is the state of tension which holds between the constituents of any situation whatever, and is an omnipresent feature of reality: ' . . . mechanical motion under external force occurs through the internal contradictoriness of things. Simple growth in plants and animals, their quantitative development, is likewise chiefly the result of their internal contradictions. Similarly, social development is due chiefly not to external but to internal causes.' (Mao Tse-tung: *On Contradiction* 1937 in *Selected Works*, Vol. I) It is the ceaseless working out of the tensions inherent in any contradiction in this sense of the term which is called *dialectical change*.

Further, Maoists (in common with other Marxists) hold that the dialectical change which is what manifests itself to us as history has a discernible direction. Because dialectical change is a universal feature of the nature of things, the direction of change can be predicted: there are laws of history in the same sense as there are laws of science. In human history, the dialectical change is fuelled by economic factors, and manifests itself as class struggle. Human history, in effect, is construed by Marxists as a relentless struggle to gain control of what they call the means of production, the source of all wealth. Those who have control of the means of production use every method in their power to retain this control and so prevent an egalitarian distribution of wealth. Central among the techniques used, wittingly or otherwise, is the inculcation in the minds of the oppressed of false beliefs which inculcate quiescent acceptance of the status quo. Among the most important of these beliefs are religious beliefs: hence Marx's much-quoted aphorism, 'Religion is the opium of the people'. Religion is in Marxist terms merely a set of false beliefs used to oppress the already dispossessed. It will be eliminated from the ideal communist state.

Only one area of thought is exempt from use as a tool of oppression in this way, and that is empirical science. This is held by Marxists to be simply objectively true. Further, Marxism itself (including its Maoist version) is held to be not a philosophy but a science on a par with physics, chemistry and so forth. Hence the laws of historical change proposed by Marxists are held to have the status of scientific laws. This is an essential move for Marxists to make if they are to avoid the logical fallacy called self-refutation. They contend that philosophies are, like religions, merely tools of oppression designed to keep the masses quiet. They must therefore regard their own views as other than merely philosophical.

With these few points in mind, it will become clear why General Tao, in chs 8–11, arrives at the conclusions he does: he praises Sun Tzu for a 'primitive' awareness of the contradictory nature of reality and of the dialectical nature of historical change; for arriving at some law-like statements about war; and for his 'atheism' (an interpretation with which I find it hard to agree, at least if one takes atheism in a broad sense to mean the absence of any form of religious dimension. Certainly, Sun did not believe in anything like the god of the monotheist religions, but the presence of the Taoist ideal of spirituality in *The Art of War* seems to me indisputable). Equally, Sun is criticised for any alleged condescension to the peasant classes, and is said to be limited by his own position in the class hierarchy. Readers will make up their own minds on these issues.

What General Tao's commentary makes abundantly clear is the continuing vitality of Sun Tzu's work. It continues to be taken very seriously, a testimony to the fact that many of its ideas have not dated. This is the mark of a true classic.

ROBERT WILKINSON

SUGGESTIONS FOR FURTHER READING

Classic Commentaries on Sun Tzu

T. Cleary (ed. and tr.), *Sun Tzu's* The Art of War, Shambhala,
Boston and London 1988
In this edition, Sun Tzu's text is interspersed with extracts
from important Chinese commentaries.

T. Cleary (ed. and tr.), *Mastering the Art of War*, Shambhala,
Boston and London 1989
Two further major commentaries on Sun Tzu.

Also referred to

R. T. Ames, *The Art of Rulership: A Study of Ancient Chinese
Political Thought*, SUNY Press, Albany 1994

Mao Tse-tung, *On Contradiction*, 1937, reprinted in *Selected
Works of Mao Tse-tung*, 4 volumes, Foreign Languages Press,
Peking (Beijing) 1967

GENERAL TAO HANZHANG'S
COMMENTARY ON THE ART OF WAR

CHAPTER 1

Strategic Considerations

The basic thesis of Sun Tzu's *The Art of War* is to try to overcome the enemy by wisdom, not by force alone. Sun Tzu believed that a military struggle was not only a competition between military forces, but also a comprehensive conflict embracing politics, economics, military force and diplomacy.

The attitude of Sun Tzu towards war is one of extreme prudence, earnestness and seriousness. He said: 'War is a matter of vital importance to the state; a matter of life or death; the road either to survival or to ruin. Hence, it is imperative that it be studied thoroughly.'

Five Fundamental Factors of War

Sun Tzu said: 'One should appraise a war first of all in terms of five fundamental factors and make comparisons of various conditions of the antagonistic sides in order to assess the outcome. The first of the fundamental factors is politics; the second, weather; the third, terrain; the fourth, the commander; and the fifth, doctrine.' In summary, Sun Tzu believed that one has to deliberate on the basic conditions which decide a war, and among them, five fundamental factors (supra) and seven elements (infra) are the primary ones.

In terms of politics, he meant that the sovereign should use political pressure or other means to bring the people into harmony with him. As for weather, he referred to the interaction of natural forces; the effects of day and night, rain and fair weather, cold and heat, time of day and seasons, and to make full use of favourable conditions and avoid any negative factors. By terrain, he meant distances, whether the ground is traversed with ease or difficulty, whether it is suitable for offensive or defensive tactics, and whether it is fit for the deployment of troops. As for the commander, he specified the general's qualities of wisdom, sincerity, benevolence, courage, tenacity, and strictness. By doctrine, he meant the discipline and organisation of troops, the assignment of appropriate ranks to officers and their respective duties, regulations, and management of logistics.

These are the fundamental factors Sun Tzu believed to be imperative for analysing and judging victory or defeat in a war. To analyse these factors, one has to answer the following questions, which were known as the 'seven elements'.

1   Which of the two sovereigns is more sagacious?
2   Which of the two commanders is wiser and more able?
3   Which of the two armies has the advantages of nature and the terrain?
4   On which side is discipline more rigorously enforced?
5   Which of the two armies is stronger?
6   Which side has the better-trained officers and men?
7   Which side administers rewards and punishments in a more enlightened manner?

After making a comprehensive analysis, one will be able to forecast which of the two sides will be victorious. Of course, from the point of view of a modern war, these conditions are obviously insufficient. It was commendable, however, for Sun Tzu to discover these fundamental factors over two thousand years ago.

During China's Anti-Japanese War, Comrade Mao Zedong wrote a brilliant military essay, 'On the Protracted War', in which, having analysed the various factors of politics, economics, military affairs, diplomacy and geography, he came to the conclusion that China would eventually be victorious over the Japanese invaders. History proved him to be right. China's enemy in a future war against aggression will be different from the Japanese, and the Chinese army will also be different. But Sun Tzu's ways of analysing a war will remain practical and significant for China's war strategies.

Sun Tzu's Strategies of War

Sun Tzu was extremely prudent as far as strategy was concerned. He considered it best to subdue the enemy's army without fighting. He pointed out: 'To win one hundred victories in one hundred battles is not the acme of skill. To subdue the enemy without fighting is the supreme excellence.' He reached this conclusion after carefully summing up the experience of past wars at that time.

Sun Tzu's principle of field operations was to take pre-emptive measures and seek quick decisions in campaigns. This principle was formulated from the historical and social conditions of that time. In his chapter entitled 'Waging War', Sun Tzu said: 'When the army engages in protracted campaigns, the resources of the state will not suffice. When your army is exhausted and its morale sinks and your treasure is spent, rulers of other states will take advantage of your distress and act. Then, even though you have wise counsellors, none will be able to make good plans for the future. Thus, though we have heard of excessive haste in war, we have not yet seen a clever operation that was prolonged.' He again pointed out in the same chapter: 'Those adept in waging war do not require a second levy of conscripts or more than two provisionings. They carry military equipment from the homeland, but rely on the enemy for provisions.'

Why are quick decisions and pre-emptive measures required in a battle? This is determined by various social conditions, especially by the economic factors prevalent at the time of war. In Sun Tzu's time, a state was smaller than a province is today. Its population was small and materials limited. Thus, it was unable to support a protracted campaign.

Marshal Liu Bocheng's Taboos of War

Marshal Liu Bocheng believed that one had to take into consideration the following five 'taboos' in making strategic decisions:

1 Do not fight a war if the country is not powerful enough (including manpower and financial and military strength).
2 Do not fight a war if the situation is unfavourable (including the international situation and the attitudes of neighbouring countries).
3 Do not fight a war if there is no domestic tranquillity.
4 Do not fight a war if the people do not support it.
5 Do not fight a war if the country has to fight on two or more fronts.

It is important to consider these five conditions in making a strategic decision, but they are not all required before a war is fought, nor are they of equal importance. The first and fifth conditions are more important than the others. Obviously, the victim of aggression should not be bound by those five taboos when it fights against the aggressor. And what is also obvious is that China should pay adequate attention to its defences when it emphasises economic construction while the international situation is still in turbulence and factors of war exist.

Marshal Liu also cited a number of examples to explain the five taboos: 'It was stupid of General Tojo [of Japan] to unleash the Pacific War in 1941. While he was unable to pull one of his legs from the mire of China, he put the other leg into Southeast Asia, thus fighting on two fronts (against China and the United States, two big powers, on the one hand, and the southeast Asian countries on the other).

'Stalin was wiser. He had tried his best to come to terms with Japan while fighting against Nazi Germany. Meeting personally with the Japanese ambassador, he repeatedly expressed his wish to keep friendly relations with Japan and abide by the mutual non-aggression treaty between the Soviet Union and Japan. He declared war on Japan only when Germany had been defeated.' There have been quite a few cases in which an army was defeated while fighting against more than one enemy; Hitler and Napoleon were only two of them.

It is always for a country's own fundamental interests and strategic posture that it make an alliance, conclude a treaty, or sign an agreement or convention with other countries after serious deliberations. After a treaty is concluded, unless it is an unequal one, it should be abided by within its period of validity; otherwise the country or leader will lose credibility in the eyes of the world. Hitler was a man of such perfidiousness.

The Art of War *in Chinese History*

Sun Tzu pointed out in *The Art of War*: 'What is of supreme importance in war is to upset the enemy's strategic plans. Next best is to disrupt his alliances by diplomacy, and the next best is to attack his army. The worst policy is to attack cities.' This principle of Sun Tzu's is the quintessence of strategic ideas, which has been greatly valued by militarists in history, and is also a general rule to be observed in all anti-aggressive wars.

Sun Tzu did not elaborate upon his idea of upsetting the enemy's strategic plans. It is, therefore, necessary to give a few examples to explain what he meant. I think that Sun Tzu had a twofold meaning: to make strategic decisions and to defeat the enemy with strategy. There have been numerous examples in China's history of war which can elaborate this principle.

THE DIALOGUE AT LONGZHONG   During the period of the Three Kingdoms [220–265 AD], Liu Bei went to the thatched cottage of Zhuge Liang three times, requesting assistance in Liu's struggle for domination of China. In *The Dialogue at Longzhong* [Shangyang County, Hubei Province], Zhuge put forward three principles which were typical strategic calculations:

1   Advance westward and occupy Sichuan as a base, and then wait for the appropriate time to advance to the Central Plains (comprising the middle and lower reaches of the Yellow River).
2   Form an alliance with the kingdom of Wu in order that the forces of (Shu) Han will not be destroyed one by one.
3   Boycott Wei (Cao Cao) in the north, thus making the political situation clear to the people, winning them to Liu's side.

Before Liu Bei asked Zhuge Liang to be his chief of staff, he had relied upon Yuan Shao to assist him. Liu Bei then went to Liu Biao for assistance without trying to have his own base. Why? This was because Liu Bei did not make a general analysis of the national situation and did not have a correct strategic decision. The Central Plains at that time were the scene of bitter struggles between various warlords. For this reason, there was hardly any possibility of Liu Bei establishing his own base there or setting up an army to fight against Cao Cao. Nor could he gain any advantage by making use of conflicts among warlords on the Central Plains.

Zhuge Liang made a thorough study in *The Dialogue at Longzhong* of the strategic position of Sichuan and came to the conclusion that Liu Bei must establish a reliable base there. Let us further analyse the three points in *The Dialogue at Longzhong*:

First, once it had Sichuan as a base, Liu Bei's army could recuperate and build up its energy before attacking the Central Plains. Sichuan, being rich in manpower and raw materials, had always been a land of abundance, and was, therefore, a reliable economic base for Liu Bei. Second, Liu Bei could avoid the danger of fighting on two fronts against Cao Cao as well as Sun Quan. Third, Liu Bei's army could take the initiative of advancing while carrying out an offensive and defending itself while retreating.

Liu Bei should make an alliance with the kingdom of Wu because at that time Wei in the north and Wu in the southeast were the only two powerful states left. To ally himself with Wu and boycott Wei would avoid fighting on two fronts and secure a peaceful environment in which to built up his strength. This policy made a clear distinction between enemies and friends.

Liu Bei should boycott Cao Cao because the power of the Han Dynasty then was, in fact, in the hands of Cao Cao, who in an attempt to put all of China under his rule gave orders to all the sovereigns in the name of the emperor. It would be politically disadvantageous not to boycott Cao Cao. Liu Bei decided to revitalise the Han Dynasty in the name of being a close relative of the monarchy. His state of Sichuan was mountainous in the north, which was excellent for defence. Therefore, Cao Cao did not dare to attack Sichuan before he had conquered the kingdom of *Wu* in the east.

The purpose of expounding the strategy as Zhuge Liang stated in *The Dialogue at Longzhong* was to prove the importance of the idea of attacking an enemy's strategy.

THE BATTLE OF KUANLIN Another typical example of subduing the enemy by wisdom occurred in 354 BC. The capital of Zhao at that time was Handan [in the present Hebei Province]; the capital of Wei was Daliang [the present Keifan in Henan Province]; and the capital of Qi was Linzi [the present Zibo in Shandong Province].

General Pang Juan of Wei directed an army of one hundred thousand men and surrounded Handan, the capital of Zhao. Zhao sent an emissary to Qi to ask for help. The sovereign of Qi summoned his generals and officials to discuss a plan to rescue Zhao. General Tien Ji offered himself as commander of a force of one hundred thousand men to fight against Pang Juan in order to rescue Zhao from the siege. But Qi's military adviser, Pang Bin, objected to it, saying that the best way of rescuing Zhao was to send an army to besiege Daliang, Wei's capital. He pointed out that the crack troops of Wei had all been sent to Handan, leaving its capital an unprotected city. When troops were sent towards Daliang, the sovereign of Wei would certainly order Pang Juan to come back and defend Daliang. The siege of Handan would be avoided without a fight. And when Pang Juan's troops were coming back to its aid, Qi's troops would choose a place to have a battle with Pang's troops to defeat them.

This stratagem was 'to attack where he is sure to come to its rescue.' It was a much better stratagem than General Tien Ji's plan to fight a battle with Pang Juan near Handan after a long and tiring march. Therefore, Qi's sovereign decided to send troops to Daliang under General Tien Ji's command, with Sun Bin as his military adviser. When Qi's troops were on their way to Daliang, the sovereign of Wei, as expected, ordered Pang Juan to hurry back to Daliang with his army. The siege of Zhao was indeed ended without a fight. While the troops of Wei were retreating to Daliang, they came across Qi's troops at Kuanlin district, and were defeated. This was called the Battle of Kuanlin. In retrospect, we can conclude that Tien Ji's plan to help Zhao was one of attacking the enemy with strength, while Sun Bin's plan was to defeat the enemy with wisdom.

THE BATTLE OF MING TIAO   In 1763 BC, Yi Ying defeated his enemy by strategic considerations after analysing the situation and weighing the advantages and disadvantages. Yi Ying was one of Sung Tang's important officials, entitled Ah Heng – an official equivalent to a prime minister and chief of staff of the army. Yi Ying made suggestions that Sung Tang should refuse to pay tributes to Xia Jie in order to test his popularity and power over his people. Sung Tang accepted this suggestion and stopped paying tributes that year. Jie was furious and dispatched troops from nine tribes to attack Tang. Since Jie was still popular among his subjects, Yi Yang advised Tang to apologise to Jie and pay more tributes to him.

The second year Tang again refused to pay tributes. Jie was even more angry and wanted again to dispatch troops from the nine tribes to Tang. But this time the tribes were not so ready to send troops, complaining that they were poor. As a result of dispatching them every year, the soldiers were weary. Only three tribes answered the call and dispatched troops. Thereupon, Yi Ying said now that Jie had lost his popularity and fighting capacity and the morale of the troops sent by three tribes was low; this was the time to fight Jie. Sung Tang followed his advice and, together with the troops of other sovereigns, lay in ambush at Ming Tiao of Anyi [in the present Shansi Province] and defeated Xia Jie there. Then Tang established the kingdom of Shang. Historically, this is known as the Battle of Ming Tiao. It is a typical example of finding an appropriate opportunity to defeat the enemy after analysing the situation.

Diplomacy

Sun Tzu attached great importance to diplomacy. He used to make alliances with forces in order to fight against a common enemy. The Wu kingdom at this time was situated at the place of the present Suzhou and Wusi. To its west was the powerful Cu kingdom [in present Hubei, Anhui and Hunan provinces]. They adjoined one another and had repeated border conflicts. Sun Tzu was eager to ally the Wu and Qi kingdoms in the north in order to alleviate pressure from that source and concentrate its forces in the fighting against Cu. The policy of disrupting an enemy's alliances in Sun Tzu's *The Art of War* is a strategy of practical importance. This means to secure an advantageous posture strategically through diplomacy. It is also the idea of defeating the enemy by strategic considerations. The following three examples will suffice to elaborate this idea.

STALIN'S NON-AGGRESSION PACT WITH HITLER   Before World War II, the Soviet Union tried its best to sign an agreement of mutual assistance with Britain and France in order to prevent the invasion of Nazi Germany. But the British and French rulers at that time attempted to direct the scourge of Germany towards the east – the Soviet Union. As a result, several talks between the three powers failed in spite of efforts made by the Soviet Union. Under the circumstances, Stalin could not have acted otherwise than to sign a non-aggression pact with Germany, which stopped the German advance for a certain period and thereby gave time for Soviet preparation. The British and French rulers were not as alert as the Soviet Union and suffered more immediately the force of Hitler's blitzkrieg. This was described by Comrade Mao Zedong as 'to lift a stone just to crush one's own feet'. Stalin's tactic of delaying the attack by Hitler through diplomatic means, thereby gaining time for preparation, was wise and desirable from a military strategic point of view.

THE DISRUPTION OF THE QI–CU ALLIANCE   During the Warring Period [475–221 BC], the kingdom of Qin wanted to attack Qi, but it feared the Qi–Cu alliance. Zhang Yi was, therefore, sent by Qin to Cu as an envoy to disrupt the Qi–Cu alliance. Upon arriving in Cu, Zhang Yi approached Queen Nan and presented her with a precious gift of pearls and jade and asked her to convey the following message to the sovereign of Cu: 'Zhang Yi has been sent to Cu as an envoy to meet the sovereign of Cu. Qin is ready to cede six hundred *li* of its territory to the kingdom of Cu. What Qin asks for from Cu is only friendship and non-aggression.'

The sovereign of Cu met with Zhang Yi, who tried all he could to persuade Cu of the advantages of being on good terms with Qin. The sovereign of Cu was overwhelmed by its offer of territory [the equivalent of two hundred miles of land] as a reward for friendship and promised to be on good terms with Qin.

The sovereign of Qi was furious when he heard about the news of reconciliation between the sovereign of Cu and Zhang Yi, which he believed to be a conspiracy against Qi. After this, Qi and Cu became enemies.

In fact, the offer of two hundred miles of territory was a deception. When the envoy of Cu went to Qin to accept the territory, Zhang Yi said that what he had promised was not two hundred miles of Qin's territory but two miles of his own property. The Cu sovereign was extremely angry when he discovered this. He sent troops to attack Qin but was defeated. From then on, the kingdom of Cu became isolated from all sides. As a result, Qin's disruption of the Qi–Cu alliance laid the foundation for the defeat of Qi and Cu, respectively.

THE ALLIANCE BETWEEN JIN AND QIN   During the Spring and Autumn Period [770–476 BC], Zheng kingdom's disruption of the alliance between Jin and Qin kingdoms while being attacked by them was another convincing example of the use of diplomacy to weaken two allies. Zheng was a small state sandwiched between the two powerful neighbouring states – Jin and Qin. Zheng, being allied with Cu, hoped Cu would come to its rescue. Being afraid of Jin's and Qin's strength, Cu dared not to send any troops. Zheng was in a desperate situation.

Zheng's sovereign then sent his veteran official, Zhu Zhiwu – an experienced diplomat who was eloquent, courageous and re-sourceful – to Qin to meet their sovereign in person. Zhu Zhiwu asked the sovereign of Qin for the reasons of its support to Jin in attacking Zheng. Qin's sovereign said he supported Jin because Zheng acted faithlessly towards Jin.

Zhu Zhiwu said: 'Zheng did break its promise with Jin, but it has always highly admired and respected the great Qin. Your Excel-lency is wise and generous. You helped Jin in its establishment of the state. Now you are again helping Jin conquer Zheng by tiring your troops on a long expedition. Zheng is far away from Qin, and you would in no way be benefited if Zheng is conquered. On the contrary, if Zheng were occupied by Jin, it is Jin that would be greatly strengthened. And since Qin and Jin are adjoined to each other, if Jin becomes even more powerful, it will surely be a potential threat to Qin. I am worried for Qin's future. Jin is not a state that is unswervingly sincere and faithful. It promised once to cede its territory west of the Huang River to Qin, but it did not keep its promise. Moreover, it dispatched troops to the border to threaten the safety of Qin. Do you like to feed a close neighbour who is a tiger? In my opinion, the best thing for Qin to do is to withdraw from this expedition and come back. This is in Qin's interest. If Qin follows my advice and withdraws its troops, Zheng is willing to be Qin's protectorate and, if necessary, provide military bases when Qin passes through the Central Plains. Zheng can also serve as a natural screen to protect Qin in the east and west against any threats from Jin.'

The sovereign of Qin was left without any argument by this ingenious remark. A tacit understanding was then reached, and Qin withdrew its troops on its own. Seeing Qin's troops being with-drawn, and being aware that Cu was an ally of Zheng and that Cu would certainly come to its defence if Zheng were attacked, Jin also withdrew its troops immediately. The siege of Zheng was thus ended without a fight. This is one of the typical examples in China's war history in which a siege was avoided thanks to diplomacy only.

Wisdom on the Battlefield

Regarding the principle of 'the next best being to attack the army', it does not mean that one should try to defeat the enemy only by force. In fact, wisdom is extremely essential on any battlefield. There have been numerous examples of the need for strategic wisdom in China's history of war.

THE BATTLE OF THE FEISHUI RIVER   In the year 383 BC, General Fu Jian of the earlier Qin Dynasty led his army southward in an attempt to conquer East Jin. Xie Xuan and Xie Shi, who were Jin generals, ordered their armies to the southern bank of the Feishui River to resist Fu Jian, whose army (numbering more than three hundred thousand) was decidedly superior to that of Jin, which numbered only eighty thousand. Obviously, Xie Xuan and Xie Shi had to defeat their enemy with wisdom.

Xie Xuan's analysis of the two armies confronting each other across the Feishui River was that Fu Jian's army was superior in number, but its command was not unified. Infantry and cavalry were mixed and the vanguard and follow-up units were far apart. Moreover, the generals in Fu Jian's army had no strategic considerations. If its vanguard units were defeated, victory would be an easy task for East Jin.

Xie Xuan surmised that if he could attack the Qin army while it was in disorder, he would surely win. Then he sent an envoy to Qin, asking them to retreat for a certain distance so that the Jin army could cross the Feishui River and fight a decisive battle with Qin. The commander of the Qin army agreed and an order was given to retreat. There naturally was some disorder in the Qin army while it retreated, owing to its weak command.

Furthermore, Zhu Xu, a Jin officer who had surrendered to the Qin army, seized the opportunity to create disorder by shouting to the follow-up units, 'The Qin army is defeated.' The Qin soldiers in the rear were fooled by this ruse, and the infantry and cavalry vied in retreating. As a result, there was great confusion in the Qin army. The Jin army, after crossing the Feishui River, took advantage of this disorder, and swiftly attacked the Qin army and defeated it. Fu Jian, commander of the Qin army, was hit by an arrow, then fled alone to the north of the Hui River on horseback. This is known as the Battle of the Feishui River.

THE BATTLE OF GAIXIA   Another example of strategic wisdom in a war occurred in the year 202 BC. The sovereign of Western Han asked Marshal Han Xin to direct the Battle of Gaixia against the Cu army, commanded by Xiang Yu, the sovereign of Western Cu. The Cu army was fairly powerful, with a force of more than ninety thousand. In addition, Xiang Yu was valiant and courageous, and no one in the Han army dared to fight him alone. Pondering the problem carefully, Han Xin decided to devise a scheme. His army laid an ambush at the Jiulishan Mountain region. He asked Li Zuoche to enrage Xiang Yu and lure his army into the ambush. To make matters worse, Han Xin sent different units to fight against Xiang Yu in turn. The Cu soldiers could get neither food nor rest. Han Xin concentrated all his forces and fought a decisive battle against Cu.

During the battle, Xiang Yu was ambushed three times, and he had to lead the army personally for more than a dozen times while attempting to escape, resulting in casualties of more than ten generals. In the end, Xiang Yu had to order a retreat because the soldiers were without food and reinforcements. Han Xin followed up his victory with a quick pursuit, not allowing Xiang Yu's men even a breathing spell. Xiang Yu committed suicide by cutting his throat. The remnants of the Cu army surrendered.

We can conclude that the Battle of Gaixia was won by Han Xin because of his correct strategy. If he had tried to win merely by force, it could have been a very different outcome, to say nothing of a complete annihilation of the Cu army.

Summary

Let us summarise what we have learned so far about Sun Tzu's theories relating to strategic considerations. At the very begunning of Sun Tzu's *The Art of War*, he pointed out: 'War is a matter of vital importance to the state; a matter of life or death, the road to survival or ruin. Hence, it is imperative that it be studied thoroughly.' Therefore, one should appraise it in terms of the five fundamental factors and compare the seven elements. One has first to analyse and deliberate on the fighting capacity and advantages and disadvantages of one's own army and of the enemy. What is required of a commander is to 'subdue the enemy troops without a fight' and to win by strategic considerations.

As we have seen, Sun Tzu advocated that in a war, generally the best policy is to attack the enemy's strategy. Next best is to disrupt his alliances by diplomacy. The next in order is to attack the enemy's army in the field, and the worst policy is to attack cities. His doctrine was that to fight a war is not only a matter of military affairs, but a matter relating to politics, economics, diplomacy, climate and geography. Only when all these factors are taken into consideration comprehensively can one defeat the enemy. He was in favour of gaining the initiative by striking first, fighting a quick battle to force a quick decision and not protracting a war. (These conclusions were reached according to the political and economic conditions in Sun Tzu's time.)

Sun Tzu believed that the state should make up the strategy of war, and the commander should organise and direct the battles. In other words, one should first devise a strategy in a safe command position that will ensure victory on whatever battlefield. All factors have to be considered practically and realistically without any wishful thinking.

Sun Tzu advocated that one should take the initiative and be flexible in fighting a war. Try to grasp the crux of the battle and attack where the enemy feels invulnerable, thus bringing about a decisive change. Then make the best use of the situation and guide the fight to victory.

Devise a strategy line with the fundamental and long-term interests of the state, not just expediency. It is much more complicated to devise a strategy than to lay a plan for a battle. One has to consider a much wider scope and take into consideration disadvantages as well as advantages, and try to develop and make use of all positive factors while reducing negative ones. (It is almost impossible totally to avoid the latter.)

Lastly, all things in the world have their strong and weak points, their advantages and disadvantages. They are dialectical and are transformed into their opposites under certain circumstances. But it is always the primary and key factor that is decisive; so one should never be misled by complicated minor factors

CHAPTER 2

Posture of Army

The chapter entitled 'Posture of Army' in Sun Tzu's *The Art of War* is a discussion of the way an army utilises its position before a battle. By posture, Sun Tzu did not mean the formation or deployment of an army during a battle, but the strategically advantageous posture before a battle that enables it to have a flexible, mobile, and changeable position during a campaign.

In discussing 'energy' or 'posture', it would appear that Sun Tzu set several necessary preliminary conditions for having the most advantageous position:

1 Those who are superior in military strength and weapons.
2 Occupation of a favourable terrain.
3 Excellent training of troops and high morale among soldiers.
4 Commanders who are resourceful, thoughtful, and good at seizing opportunities for combat.

A good posture is not inherent but comes from excellent art of direction of war, rich experience in combat, and thoughtfulness in strategy and tactics on the part of the commanders. Sun Tzu pointed out:

'The energy of troops skilfully commanded in battle can be compared to the momentum of round boulders which roll down from a mountain thousands of feet in height . . . When torrential water tosses boulders, it is because of its momentum; when a hawk strikes swiftly and breaks the body of its prey, it is because of timing. Thus, the momentum of a good commander is overwhelming and his attack precisely timed.'

A brilliant commander seeks victory from the effect of combined energy and does not demand too much of his men. He selects his men and they exploit the situation. He should not only be skilful in employing various strategic considerations in order to change the disadvantages into advantages, he should also be good at creating momentum and regulating his troops, so that the attack can be both extremely swift and vigorous.

Generally speaking, those who are superior in military strength and weapons usually have an advantageous posture. But this is not universal. Sometimes one who is inferior can also be in an advantageous posture if he makes use of the situation and all the advantages that he has.

For instance, in southern China, there is a small animal, a kind of leopard cat, which is the same size as a cat. It is much weaker in strength than a tiger, but it often attacks a tiger when it sees one. It is as nimble as a squirrel and usually lays an ambush in a tree, and suddenly jumps on to the back of the tiger, gets hold of the tiger's tail, and uses its sharp paw to vigorously scratch the tiger's anus. The tiger jumps and roars from pain, but it is unable to reach the leopard cat. The only solution is for the tiger to roll on the ground, at which time the small animal flees rapidly.

The kingfisher is a small bird of 15 centimetres long with green feathers and a sharp beak like a nail. It usually flies over water. When it sees a fish, it draws its wings in and dashes into the water with all its force like an arrow. Sometimes it can catch a fish bigger than itself. The action of a kingfisher fully illustrates what Sun Tzu stated: 'the momentum is overwhelming and attack precisely timed.'

Operational Research

In ancient Chinese history, there is a story about a horse race between the sovereign of Qi (Qi Wei Wang) and General Tien Ji, in which Sun Bin assisted Tien Ji to win by exercising the concept of 'operational research'. Sun was aware of how his advice worked but ignorant of why.

Tien Ji often had horse races with the sovereign of Qi, but lost each time because Qi's horses were better. Qi's best horses ran 45 *li* per hour [equal to about 15 miles per hour], while Tien Ji's ran 43 *li*; Qi's next-best horses ran 41 *li*, Tien Ji's ran 40; Qi's worst horses ran 38 *li*, Tien Ji's ran 36 *li*. In each race, Tien Ji employed the same category of horses to race against the sovereign of Qi, and lost in each. Upon learning this, Sun Bin suggested to Tien Ji that he first use his worst horses to race with Qi's best ones, a race he would no doubt lose. In the second race, Tien Ji should use his best horses to race with Qi's next-best ones, which would mean 43 *li* v. 40 *li*, for a race he would surely win. In the third race, he should use his next-best horses against Qi's worst ones, 40 *li* v. 38 *li*, and he would again win. Then Tien Ji would win two out of three races and be the overall winner.

Operational research has not yet been popularised in the sphere of war. It will be a science of how best to employ one's force when it is applied in the sphere of military science.

The Element of Surprise

A commander who possesses wisdom and courage should try his best to have an overwhelming momentum and take prompt action in a campaign. He should rely not only on his superior strength but also on all the advantageous factors so that he may be able to defeat his enemy with a surprise move.

There have been many examples in the history of the Chinese army during different periods of the Revolution when it was in an inferior position strategically, but was able to defeat the enemy by concentrating its forces on the offensive. It all depends on a commander's resourcefulness and flexibility to seize an opportunity in which he may be able to have overwhelming momentum and take prompt action. Battles fought by the First Field Army at Qinghua Bian, Yangmahe and Yichuan in the 1940s were such examples. There are also many examples one can find in battles fought by other field armies. And most of them share the following common characteristics:

1 Flexibility in moving troops and skilfulness in seizing opportunities to fight.
2 Concentration of forces to defeat the enemies one by one.
3 Swiftness in moving troops and a comparatively short time spent in a battle.
4 Annihilation of enemies in one movement.

There are many factors which lead to advantageous posture for an army. For example, the terrain. In China, there is a saying: 'With only one man guarding the mountain pass, ten thousand men are not able to pass.' This does not mean that a single man can fight against ten thousand persons, but he who occupies an advantageous position can resist the attack of ten thousand men.

To take the enemy by surprise is another factor. In the East Han

Dynasty, Emperor Guangwu attacked the rear of Wang Mang's army by surprise with his five thousand soldiers and defeated it. This is a typical case.

To gain initiative and be flexible is another important factor. For instance, strike first whenever possible, and force the enemy into passivity. Attack promptly where the enemy is most vulnerable. Try to occupy a location of command that offers a good overall view of the battlefield.

Sun Tzu wrote in the chapter entitled 'Manoeuvring': 'Close to the field of battle, they await an enemy coming from afar; at rest, they await an exhausted enemy; with well-fed troops, they await hungry ones . . . Avoid the enemy when its spirit is keen and attack it when it is sluggish and the soldiers are homesick . . . Do not engage an enemy advancing with well-ordered banners, nor one whose formations are in impressive array.'

Summary

The following is a summary of Sun Tzu's thoughts regarding military posture:

Energy and favourable posture of an army come from the strategic considerations of commanders. A good commander must be deft at following Sun Tzu's principles: 'Know the enemy and know yourself; in a hundred battles you will never be defeated.' 'Attack where the enemy is not guarded and catch him by surprise.' 'Defeat your enemy by a surprise move.' 'Attack the enemy at a place where the enemy is sure to come to its rescue.'

A commander should try to move troops with overwhelming momentum and prompt action; he should have troops moving swiftly and fighting courageously.

A commander should have a correct understanding of a battle, and development of a campaign, and try to seize upon a favourable opportunity for fighting.

A commander should establish superiority of his army over the enemy's in number and in quality. (It is difficult to have an overall superiority, but to have partial advantages is possible.)

A commander should make use of advantageous terrains to make up for a lack of soldiers. Terrain can restrict the mobility of the enemy, which can even put it in a fatal position. However, if a good terrain is not properly made use of, the result will be catastrophic.

CHAPTER 3

Extraordinary and Normal Forces

Since the publication of Sun Tzu's *The Art of War*, military scholars have devised many explanations of the 'extraordinary and normal forces'. In the book *Sun Tzu as Annotated by Eleven Scholars* (Sung Dynasty Edition), one of the annotators, Wei Liaozi, said: 'The forces sent first to confront the enemy are normal ones, and sent later to attack the enemy are extraordinary ones.' Cao Cao said something to the same effect.

In *A Dialogue Between Tang and Li,* Tang Taizong told Li Jing: 'My normal forces would seem extraordinary to the enemy, and my extraordinary seem normal. That is exactly what is called deception. Extraordinary forces appear to be normal and normal, extraordinary; changes are unpredictable.'

Li Jing also commented on the victory of the Battle of Huo Yi: 'It would have been impossible for us to win, if normal forces had not been disguised as extraordinary and extraordinary as normal. Therefore, it all depends on the commander, who decides how and when to use normal force or extraordinary.'

Commenting on the subject, Marshal Liu Bocheng explained: 'The normal forces and extraordinary forces are a dialectical unity, of which all generals must have a good grasp. Extraordinary forces contain normal ones, and normal, extraordinary. There should be unpredictable changes in them . . . What are the normal forces? Generally speaking, forces which fight in a regular way according to usual tactical principles are normal forces. Forces which fight otherwise and move stealthily and attack the enemy by surprise are extraordinary ones.'

Sun Tzu did not devote a separate chapter to the subject of the normal and extraordinary forces, but he included it in the chapter entitled 'Posture of Army'. For instance, he wrote: 'There are unending changes of the normal and extraordinary forces. They end and recommence – cyclical, as are the movements of the sun and moon. They die away and are reborn – recurrent, as are the passing seasons. Generally, in battle, use the normal force to engage the enemy and the extraordinary to win. Therefore, the resources of those skilled in the use of extraordinary forces are as infinite as the heavens and earth, as inexhaustible as the flow of the great rivers . . . It is the skilful operation of the extraordinary and the normal forces that make an army capable of sustaining the enemy's attack without suffering defeat.'

It must be pointed out that Sun Tzu's use of the word 'cyclical' seems to imply 'cyclicalism'. However, a careful study of the context would reveal that he used it as a metaphor to describe the changeability and unpredictability of employing extraordinary and normal forces. It is in no way related to cyclicalism and metaphysics, which denies the spiral development of all things.

Extraordinary Forces in History

There have been numerous examples of battles in Chinese history in which victory has been achieved by catching the enemy by surprise.

THE FORMATION OF OXEN WITH FIRE   In the year 279 BC, Qi's general, Tian Dan, was besieged in the city of Jimo. In order to save the kingdom of Qi, Tian Dan thought of a scheme. He collected more than a thousand oxen and covered each of them with a colourful cloth, then tied sharp daggers on their horns and dried reeds dipped in oil on their tails. He assembled five thousand soldiers all disguised as monsters. When night fell and the soldiers of the Yen army were all sound asleep, he lit the reeds on the oxen's tails. The oxen dashed towards the camps of the Yen army followed by Tian Dan's five thousand soldiers. The Yen army was caught by surprise and thrown into utter chaos. In this battle, Yen's troops were totally wiped out, and thereafter the victorious Tian Dan recaptured more than seventy cities in succession. The kingdom of Qi was saved from conquest. The battle was called the 'Formation of Oxen with Fire', and has become a famous example of taking the enemy by surprise.

THE CAMPAIGN TO OUTFLANK SHU   In the year 263 AD, in the late period of the Three Kingdoms, General Deng Ai of the kingdom of Wei was asked to attack the kingdom of Shu. Normally they had to attack Jianman Pass first. Knowing the pass was strongly fortified, Deng Ai directed his ten thousand troops to outflank the enemy. They marched along small paths in the Yingping Mountain Valley, crossing about two hundred miles of no-man's-land and even tunnelling through mountains. When they came to the perilous Mage Mountain, there was not even a path. He wrapped his body with a blanket and rolled down the mountain at the head of his men. Then his men came down one after another with the help of ropes, and quickly occupied Jiangyou Pass, and soon after, the city of Mianzu. They advanced swiftly and reached Chengdu in November, taking the enemy by surprise. Liu Shan, general of Shu, was forced to surrender. This battle has been known for its suddenness and unexpectedness.

THE BATTLE OF GUAN DU   In the year 200 AD the troops of Cao Cao and Yuan Shao met in a confrontation at Guan Du. Yuan's troops were well provisioned and therefore able to withstand a protracted war, while Cao's troops ran short of provisions and could only fight a quick battle. Cao Cao was at his wits' end and very worried. Then Xu You, one of Yuan's counsellors who committed crimes and feared prosecution, joined sides with Cao Cao, who was pleased to accept him.

At their meeting, Cao Cao said: 'I want to defeat Yuan's army in a quick strike, but I think I am not able to do so because of the big gap in our strength. I am thinking of retreating but afraid of pursuit by Yuan's army. I hope you can give me counsel.'

Xu asked Cao: 'What do you think is the key problem in the battlefield?'

Cao said: 'Yuan Shao can fight a protracted war because his provisions are abundant, while we cannot because of our poor provisions.'

'So the key problem is provisions,' said Xu. 'Yuan's army stored their rations at Wucao, guarded only by a small force. You should raid Wucao and burn their provisions, which would surely result in chaos in Yuan's army.'

Cao Cao followed his advice, raided Wucao, and burnt almost all the provisions of Yuan's army. On learning about it, Yuan's troops were thrown into great confusion and soon retreated in disorder. Cao's troops pursued the chaotic Yuan army and defeated it. In this single battle, hundreds of thousands of Yuan's troops were destroyed. After that, Cao again defeated Yuan at Cang Ting.

Consequently, Yuan Shao died from a disease. His two sons fought for the throne and were both killed by Cao Cao. Since then, Cao consolidated his base in the northern area of the Central Plains and laid a solid foundation for the conquest of the whole Central Plains. As a result, the key to victory in a campaign sometimes does not lie in the battlefield but in devising apt strategies. This is another example of catching the enemy by surprise, which is called the scheme of 'taking away the firewood from under the cauldron'.

These are examples of employing extraordinary forces. Similar ones were numerous in the history of the People's Liberation Army (PLA). From them, we can say that Wei Liaozi's annotation might not be correct – that labelling a force normal or extraordinary has nothing to do with which occurs first. Deng Ai's extraordinary crossing of Yingping Mountain Valley occurred before the real campaign started, as did the burning of Yuan's provisions by Cao Cao at Wucao. The 'Formation of Oxen with Fire' was arranged by Tian Dan to break the siege of the city of Jimo. Therefore, the extraordinary forces are used to take the enemy by surprise regardless of when they occur in time. We can safely say that Deng Ai did something normal contained in the extraordinary. Tian Dan's formation of oxen was something extraordinary contained in the normal.

During the Hui Hai campaign launched by the PLA in 1948, the fights between the Chinese military corps and the enemy troops were considered normal forces, but they also involved the use of extraordinary forces, such as Sun Tzu wrote: 'to besiege a place to annihilate the enemy relief force', and 'to make a feint to the east and attack in the west'. Therefore, we say there were unending changes of the normal and extraordinary forces.

The extraordinary and normal forces are a dialectical unity and they are interchangeable. Normal forces can be turned into extraordinary ones in accordance with the changes in the field, and vice versa. Some of the commanders did not employ troops according to normal principles, such as 'fighting with one's back to the river' or 'cutting off all means of retreat', but they won.

The employment of troops should be subject to variations. The same military principle can be applied in different ways. In Chinese history, there have been a number of wars; some lasting hundreds of years (the Spring and Autumn Warring Period), others lasting dozens of years (the anti-imperialist and anti-feudal wars in the contemporary period). The natures of these wars were obviously different; so were the ways of fighting. But many of Sun Tzu's principles and theories of war were applied in various ways in these conflicts. For instance: making correct estimates before engaging in battles; the deft application of strategic considerations; catching the enemy by surprise; taking initiative into one's hand; knowing the enemy and knowing yourself; concentrating large numbers of troops to fight a much smaller unit of the enemy. In short, as Sun Tzu pointed out: 'Ingenuity in varying tactics depends on mother wit.'

Summary

To summarise Sun Tzu's position on the use of extraordinary and normal forces:

Employment of troops must be extraordinary and varied so that the opponents cannot predict the movement of each other's army. Sun Tzu said, 'War is a matter of deception.' That is to say, always attempt to throw your opponent into confusion.

Always try to catch the enemy by surprise. Use your troops at a place and time which are unexpected. Always try to strike a deadly blow at the enemy's weak point.

For the sake of extraordinary employment of troops, begin from a firm and unconquerable position. And then you should be far-sighted, circumspect, courageous and careful at the same time. Be able to move swiftly and to cope with any contingency.

Extraordinary and normal forces have interchangeable elements that resemble each other. This is dialectic in military affairs. You must avoid absolutes and not rigidly adhere to principles or articles in a military book. On the contrary, you should be flexible in applying them. Remember that there is no universal principle that leads to victory in every confrontation.

CHAPTER 4

Void and Actuality

In various chapters of Sun Tzu's *The Art of War* many important principles are given to guide the movement of an army. In the chapter entitled 'Void and Actuality', Sun Tzu did not elaborate on this subject. Nevertheless, the major principles in it are immortal. For instance, he pointed out: 'In making tactical dispositions, the acme is to leave no ascertainable shape. Then the most penetrating spies cannot pry, nor can the wisest enemy lay any successful plans against you . . . Appear at places that the enemy must hasten to defend; move swiftly to places where you are least expected.'

In the chapter entitled 'Manoeuvring', he wrote: 'In war, practise deception and you will win victory. Move when it is advantageous to you. Concentrate or disperse your troops according to circumstances. When campaigning, move as swiftly as the wind; when marching, be leisurely, majestic and compact as the forest; in raiding and plundering, be like fire; in stationing, be firm as a mountain; when hidden, be unfathomable as the clouds; when striking, fall like a thunderbolt.

'Avoid the enemy when its spirit is keen, and attack it when it is sluggish and the soldiers are homesick. This is the art of controlling the moral factor. In good order, he awaits an enemy in disorder; in serenity, an enemy in clamorousness. This is the art of controlling the mental factor. Close to the field of battle he awaits an enemy coming from afar; at rest, he awaits an exhausted enemy; with well-fed troops, he awaits hungry ones. This is the art of controlling the physical factor. He does not engage an enemy advancing with well-ordered banners, nor one whose formations are in impressive array. This is the art of changing with the circumstances.'

In the chapter entitled 'The Nine Varieties of Ground', he said: 'Throw the soldiers into a perilous situation and they can survive;

put them on death ground and they can live.' In the chapter entitled 'Estimates', he pointed out: 'Attack the enemy where he is not prepared and where you are least expected.' All these are important principles in war.

In ancient China, many books on the art of war discussed the problem of void and actuality. Some compared them to yin and yang, meaning 'void' is 'yin' and therefore something false, and 'actuality' is 'yang', something true. This analogy is incorrect, or at least not precise. As a matter of fact, sometimes there is real action in 'void', but most of the actions are deceptive. There are actions or movements which seem to begin from weakness, but they are to deceive and trap the enemy.

Void and Actuality in War

Usually, there should be substance to any 'void' movement so that you won't be defeated. It will amount to useless adventure if there is no solid backing. In military affairs, there are also constants (something solid or actual) and variables (void). Generally speaking, constants are dominant.

The following are a few examples of war to elaborate the application of 'void and actuality'.

THE EMPTY CITY SCHEME During the period of Three Kingdoms, the kingdom of Shu lost Jieting to Wei. Soon after, the Wei army, under the command of Sima Yi, advanced straight to the West City, which was an important place strategically, but not guarded because of Shu's lack of forces. Zhuge Liang knew he could not afford to lose the West City, which would have meant a total collapse of the Shu army. Being well aware that Sima Yi was suspicious and a coward, Zhuge Liang decided to create the illusion of an empty city, which scared Sima Yi and made him withdraw his army for thirteen miles. This action won time for Zhuge Liang so that he could await reinforcements.

The 'Empty City Scheme' is not recorded in history books, but it appears in the notes of *The History of the Three Kingdoms*. Even if the story were not true, it would make sense. It tells us how to apply 'void' and 'actuality' in war. In this example, Zhuge Liang used the form of 'void' to hint at the existence of his solid backing which he didn't have. He accomplished his purpose of scaring away Sima Yi's army. As a matter of fact, since he was not backed up by force, it was an adventurist policy.

THE BATTLE OF SHIJIAZHUAN   There is a similar more recent example of void and actuality in the history of the People's Liberation Army. In October 1948, Guomindang's General Hu Yi concentrated his 94th Army and three other divisions, including several thousand trucks, in an attempt to stage a quick raid at Shijiazhuan, which was then guarded only by two garrison and training regiments of the PLA. In addition, there were three PLA regiments of the local army blocking Guomindang's advance north of Wuan County. Evidently it was not possible to stop the raid. Therefore, the commanders of the Jingcaji military area thought of a new variation of an 'empty city scheme' and took the following measures.

First of all, the PLA spokesman of the military area declared on the radio that they were aware of and prepared for Guomindang's attempt to raid Shijiazhuan. He implied that if the army were to attack, they would not be able to retreat, which suggested the PLA's imaginary strength. Hu Yi listened carefully to the broadcast, then read it in writing. He had the same nature as Sima Yi – suspicious and cowardly. He became hesitant and asked his troops to advance carefully. Thus, the advance was slowed down.

Next, the commander of the military area ordered the local units to block the enemy's advance as far as possible north of Wuan County. He also ordered the defending troops of Shijiazhuan to build fortifications along the Futou River to show that they were well prepared for the attack. In the meantime, the commander ordered the army stationed below Changjiakou to move south to reinforce Shijiazhuan. And finally, the commander ordered the sixth column to wipe out the 49th Division sent by Yen Xishan to assist Hu Yi in raiding Shijiazhuan, thus cutting off the reinforcements for Hu Yi.

Several days later, Hu Yi was all the more restless, upset, and hesitant in regard to the direction he should take. He ordered his air force to carry out aerial reconnaissance missions over Shijiazhuan and discovered that the PLA was building fortifications along the Futou and Sha Rivers (in fact, they were false fortifications), and the city of Shijiazhuan was quiet.

Three days later, Hu Yi again ordered aerial reconnaissance missions and discovered that PLA troops were moving south near Yi County to reinforce Shijiazhuan, stretched as far as one hundred miles. He estimated them to number from eighty to one hundred thousand men from the crack troops of the PLA field army. Hu Yi calculated that this reinforcement would arrive before his army did. In the meantime, he learned of the destruction of the 49th Division sent by Yen Xishan. Finally, he ended the planned raid on Shijiazhuan and the city was saved.

For its defence, the PLA devised an 'empty city scheme', which was weak in fact, but apparently strong enough to slow down the enemy's advance. At the same time, they ordered troops to come down from the north to reinforce Shijiazhuan. Zhuge Liang's use of this scheme was adventurist, but the Battle of Shijiazhuan had solid backup. It was absolutely safe.

THE BATTLE OF MALIN PASS   In the year 341 BC, the kingdom of Wei sent troops under the command of Pong Juan to attack Han. Han resisted with all its troops and fought five battles but was defeated. Han had to seek help from Qi. The sovereign of Qi sent troops to assist Han with Tian Ji in command and Sun Bin as chief of staff. Qi's troops advanced towards Ta Liang, Wei's capital, forcing Wei's army to withdraw from Han.

The sovereign of Wei sensed that Qi represented a serious threat to Wei, and there would be no peace for him if Qi were not defeated. He decided to concentrate all his crack troops with Pong Juan and Prince Shen as commanders to have a decisive battle with Qi.

Being aware of this, Qi decided not to fight Wei. Sun Bin advised Tian Ji: 'Wei's troops are famous for their bravery and usually look down upon Qi. We should pretend to fear them. According to Sun Tzu's *The Art of War*, in a forced march of one hundred *li*, the commander of the van will fall, and after fifty *li* only half the army will arrive.' He suggested that Qi should withdraw its army in order to lure the enemy inside its territory, and at the same time, increase the number of soldiers while decreasing the number of cooking stoves. In other words, Qi should first pretend to be weak and then seize an appropriate moment to catch the enemy by surprise. Tian Ji accepted his proposal.

Wei's army pursued Qi's troops all the way, and Wei's scouts reported the first day that Qi had one hundred thousand cooking stoves; the second day, fifty; and the third day, only twenty. Pong Juan believed that there were a great number of deserters in Qi's army, so he ordered the Wei army to march with even quicker speed. He personally led several thousand soldiers and advanced day and night without rest. When they came to Malin Pass, they fell into the ambush of Qi's troops and were wiped out. Pong Juan himself was captured. Qi's troops then attacked Prince Shen's troops on the crest of their victory and captured him. Since then, Qi became the largest kingdom in the north. This is a typical example of adopting the form of 'void' while being strong.

Summary

To summarise Sun Tzu's concept of void and actuality:

In employing troops, there must be interchangeable elements of 'actuality' in 'void', and 'void' in 'actuality'. Normally, it is easier to adopt the form of 'void' while being strong than from a weak position.

It is extremely important to know the characteristics of the enemy and its commander. It is also necessary to know the strong points of your various commanders so that you may ask them to do tasks for which they are best suited.

When you want to adopt the form of 'void', do it reasonably, and there must be strength (solid backing) behind it (unlike Zhuge Liang's 'Empty City Scheme'). You should take the initiative in your own hands, and adopt carefully worked-out measures.

When you want to simulate an appearance, do it cleverly and reasonably so that the enemy is confused. Try to lure the enemy in deeply.

'Void' and 'actuality' are interchangeable and limited by time. It is often difficult to see through the enemy's changes. Therefore, it is essential to have wise, active, flexible, courageous and careful commanders.

CHAPTER 5

Initiative and Flexibility in War

Sun Tzu attached great importance to gaining the initiative in any confrontation. His principles of taking pre-emptive measures, of fighting a quick battle to force a quick decision, bringing the enemy to the battlefield instead of being brought there by him, are all for the sake of gaining the initiative in a war.

Mao Zedong said: 'Losing the initiative means to be defeated, to be annihilated.' Mao Zedong advocated that in fighting a battle you must bring the enemy where you want him to be, not run after him. He thought it better to gain mastery by striking only after the enemy has made the first move so that you may ascertain the enemy's weak points.

Initiative also means mobility and flexibility for the army. It means when it attacks, it is irresistible; when it defends, it is impregnable; and when it retreats, the enemy does not dare to pursue. There are many important statements to this effect in Sun Tzu's *The Art of War*.

In the chapter entitled 'Void and Actuality', Sun Tzu wrote: 'An army may be compared to water, for water in its natural flowing avoids the heights and hastens downwards. So in a war, an army should avoid strength and strike at weakness. As water shapes its flow in accordance with the nature of the ground, an army manages to be victorious in relation to the enemy it is facing. As water retains no constant shape, so in war there are no constant conditions. One who can modify his tactics in accordance with the enemy's situation and succeed in gaining victory may be called divine.'

In regard to 'Manoeuvring', he stated: 'In war, practise deception and you will win victory. Move when it is advantageous to you. Concentrate or disperse your troops according to circumstances.'

Writing about 'Terrain', Sun Tzu said: 'The general who is experienced in war once in motion is clear in his destination and never bewildered; once he acts, his resources are limitless and his tactics varied. Therefore, I say: Know the enemy, know yourself, and your victory will never be endangered. Know the ground, know the weather, and your victory will be complete.'

In referring to 'Offensive Strategy', he wrote: 'Know the enemy and know yourself, and in a hundred battles you will never be defeated. If you know only yourself, not the enemy, your chances of winning and losing are equal. If you are ignorant of either the enemy or yourself, you will surely be defeated in every battle.'

The chapter entitled 'The Nine Variables' pointed out: 'A general who does not understand the advantages of the nine variable factors will not be able to use the terrain to his advantage, even though he is well acquainted with it. A general who directs troops and does not understand the tactics suitable to the nine variable situations will be unable to employ the troops effectively, even if he understands the "five advantages".' He emphasised in this chapter: 'For this reason, a wise general in his deliberations always considers both favourable and unfavourable factors. By taking the favourable factors into account, he makes his plan and decision feasible; by taking into account the unfavourable, he may avoid disasters.'

Sun Tzu's 'The Nine Varieties of Ground' pointed out: 'The skilful commander may be likened to *shuai-ran*, which is a kind of snake that is found in the Chang Mountains. When this snake is struck on the head, its tail attacks; when struck on the tail, its head attacks; and when struck in the centre, both head and tail attack . . . Therefore, exhibit the coyness of a maiden, until the enemy loses his alertness and gives you an opening, then move as swiftly as a hare, and the enemy will be unable to resist you.'

While being aware of the disposition of an army, and of the extraordinary and normal forces, one must at the same time gain initiative and flexibility in employing troops. Sun Tzu wisely observed: 'As water retains no constant shape, so in war there are no constant conditions.' He meant there should be no fixed formulae for employing troops. One will surely be defeated by trying to apply one particular way of fighting to different situations or using a certain tactic derived from a specific instance for complicated battles. The way of staging a suitable campaign in a mountainous and forested area may not be applicable on the plains, and vice versa. Therefore, one should try to study and create new ways of fighting in accordance with the facts of each practical situation that presents itself.

The most important principle for directing a war is that there is no shortcut to master its laws. In a battlefield, events change quickly and often appear to be unpredictable. In fact, if one uses the theory of dialectical materialism in observing and analysing the essence of war one will discover that (whether on the offensive or defensive, with strong forces or weak) there are always two sides to a question, which are closely related and transform themselves into their opposites under certain conditions. Therefore, only when a commander engages in a war can he gain insight into the objective factors that promote this transformation of opposites, and avoid disadvantages and make correct decisions leading to victory.

Deftness, Fierceness, and Swiftness in War

In this respect, Marshal Liu Bocheng stresses deftness, fierceness, and swiftness. He said: 'Flexibility in employing troops is reflected by taking measures of void or actuality deftly, such as making a feint to the east and attacking in the west, changes in the extraordinary and normal forces, diverting the enemy as you wish and making him take what you want to give, and attacking where the enemy is sure to come to the rescue and where it is most unexpected.'

THE BATTLE OF THE CHESHUI RIVER   One of Mao Zedong's most valuable attributes was his initiative and flexibility in directing a war. He often defeated his enemy by a surprise move. The Battle of the Cheshui River during the Long March was a typical example.

The Cheshui River winds through the borders of Yunnan, Guizhou and Sichuan Provinces. In January 1935, Mao Zedong decided that the Red Army should march northward from Zunyi (by way of Tongzi, Songkan, and Tucheng) and then cross the Cheshui River. The enemy was very worried about this movement. The pursuing Central Army and the provincial troops of Sichuan, Guizhou, and Hunan quickly concentrated in that area, trying to encircle the Red Army.

Aware that it was now impossible to cross the Yangzi River,

Mao Zedong ordered the Red Army to assemble in that area and await new opportunities. When he found out that the enemy in Guizhou Province was weak, he ordered the army to advance suddenly eastward, crossing the Cheshui River again, and went back to attack Tongzi and Zunyi [both in Guizhou Province] again. During the march, the Red Army annihilated twenty regiments of the enemy. Jiang Jieshi was extremely annoyed by the defeat and moved troops again in a new attempt to besiege the Red Army in the Zunyi Area.

In order to confuse and then move the enemy troops, Mao Zedong ordered the Red Army to march through Renhui and cross the Cheshui River for the third time at Maotai; then he advanced northward to southern Sichuan. Seeing this movement, Jiang Jieshi believed that the Red Army would cross the Yangzi River again and join forces with the Fourth Front Army. So he ordered the provincial troops of Sichuan, Guizhou, and Hunan and the Central Army to encircle the Red Army again in an attempt to wipe them out in a single strike.

Judging that the enemy was being moved according to his plan, Mao Zedong diverted the Red Army to turn suddenly east, crossing the Cheshui River for the fourth time, and, in a rapid march along the right wing of the enemy troops, crossed the Wujiang River and marched towards Guiyang [the capital of Guizhou]. While the main force of the Red Army feigned an attack on the capital, other troops broke through the area between Guiyang and Lungli, crossing the Hunan–Guizhou Highway, advancing towards Kuanming [the capital of Yunnan Province].

Discovering that they had been taken in, the enemy marched over 300 miles to come back to defend Kuanming. By this time, the Red Army had already crossed the Jingsa River with seven small boats in nine days and nights, reaching Huili in Sichuan. Thus, the Red Army had extricated itself from the pursuit and encirclement tactics of the Guomindang troops and realised its strategic aim of crossing the Yangzi River and going to the north of China.

From the above example, we can see Mao Zedong's masterful use of flexible tactics and excellent art of war. He directed the operations of the Red Army with miraculous skill, often beyond the expectations of the enemy. The Red Army advanced in great strides, puzzling and directing the enemy, making them weary and finally succeeding in freeing itself from their pursuit.

Mao Zedong's example illustrates the importance of selecting proper generals. An inadequate commander may succeed in one action but may well lose the overall situation. It is because he cannot adapt himself to radical changes in the field and, therefore, is unable to put into effect his superior's strategic intention. For example, during the period of the Three Kingdoms, Zhuge Liang could well be called an effective chief of staff who was good at tactical planning, but he made a mistake in assigning Ma Su as a general for the defence of Jie Ting. Ma Su had some military knowledge; however, he lacked the ability to take charge of the overall situation, and did not have the experience of employing troops flexibly. He was, in fact, a pedant.

THE BATTLE OF JINGZHOU   During the period of the Three Kingdoms, Jingzhou was occupied by the kingdom of Shu and was garrisoned by the famous general Guan Yu. The kingdom of Wu had tried to reclaim its possession of Jingzhou but had been unsuccessful. In 219 AD, the sovereign of Wu, following General Lu Meng's advice, made an agreement with Cao Cao to attack Jingzhou from the north and south simultaneously (Cao's army from the north to be led by General Cao Ren; Wu's army from the south to be led by Lu Sun).

At first, Lu Sun's army was led by Lu Meng, who was well known for his resourcefulness and bravery. Guan Yu was most cautious regarding him. Lu Meng thought of a scheme of luring the enemy away from its base. He pretended to go back to Jianye because of illness and recommended that Lu Sun take his place. When Guan Yu heard the news, he was relieved. Thinking that Lu Sun was a young general who had not much fighting experience, Guan Yu attacked Shangyang and Fancheng in the north with crack troops led by him personally, leaving Mi Fang and Fu Shireng to guard Jingzhou.

When Lu Meng learned all this, he knew his scheme was successful. He ordered several hundred men disguised as merchants to go to the northern boundary between the kingdoms of Zhu and Wu and strike at the fortresses along the river with many troops, forcing Mi Fang and his men to surrender.

However, the northward advance of Guan Yu's troops progressed smoothly. They captured Xiangyang and threatened the city of Fancheng. Yu Jing and Pang De, Cao Cao's senior generals, were both captured, and large numbers of their troops were annihilated. Cao Cao was panic-stricken and began to think about moving his capital.

Guan Yu was bitterly remorseful when he learned that Jingzhou had been attacked and taken by the Wu army. He immediately withdrew his troops and retreated towards Maicheng where he was besieged by the Wu army. Guan Yu fell into an ambush and was captured.

Lu Meng's scheme of luring the enemy away from its base was successful because he knew Guan Yu was arrogant and had a fondness for the grandiose. Lu Meng asked Lu Sun to take his place in order to completely disarm Guan Yu psychologically. The way Guan Yu led all his troops northward was a manifestation of his desire for honour. It is extremely important for a commander to know the characteristics of his opponents' generals and try every means to win the battle with strategy.

THE LIAOXI–SHENYANG CAMPAIGN During the Chinese War of Liberation [1945–49], the tactical situation in the northeastern battlefield under Lin Biao was unfavourable as a whole to the PLA. He had besieged Changchun and crossed the Songhua Jiang River three times, but had not gained the initiative or flexibility in the campaign. although his forces were superior to Wei Lihuang's, the Guomindang general. In the opinion of the PLA's Mao Zedong and Zhou Enlai, this was because of errors made by the PLA commander in that region.

After deep deliberation, Mao Zedong and Zhou Enlai decided to attack Jingzhou, which was considered a strategic move whereby the enemy would be obliged to defend a valuable position. Jingzhou was the key junction for the passage of supplies between northern and northeastern China. If Jingzhou were taken, supplies for the Guomindang army in the northeast region would be cut off. Moreover, the mutual strategic support of the enemy forces in the northern and northeastern regions would also be lost. If Jingzhou were attacked by the PLA, the enemy would be forced by the PLA's initiative to come to its rescue in a strategically weak position. If reinforcements were sent, the Guomindang army would run the risk of being wiped out while they were in motion, thus creating the conditions for the PLA to move troops flexibly.

History proved the correctness of the decision made by Mao Zedong and Zhou Enlai. Just as expected, when Jingzhou was being attacked by the PLA, reinforcements were sent from northern China by the enemy, but were intercepted by the PLA and failed to reach Jingzhou. The Guomindang troops were also dispatched from Shenyang to rescue Jingzhou and were intercepted and annihilated at Dahushan. Later, the enemy in Changchun had to surrender. In this campaign, a total of more than 470,000 Guomindang troops were wiped out. The whole of the northeastern region was liberated.

It can be concluded that strategic initiative is not innate in a battle, but has to be created by wise commanders. Flexibility of tactics in a campaign is generally obtained on the basis of strategic initiative. The Liaoxi-Shenyang campaign illustrates the truth of this theory.

Summary

Grasp the key point which affects the whole campaign: deftness, fierceness and swiftness should be understood correctly. Deftness means that a plan is put into execution craftily; fierceness is an overwhelming superiority of force, as a fierce tiger springs upon a goat; swiftness means that a battle is ended as suddenly as a flash of lightning.

Initiative and flexibility require that feints and strikes be varied, moves of the enemy be planned and directed. Attack where the enemy will surely come to its own rescue, and have several feasible alternatives in hand before starting a campaign.

Initiative in a campaign is not innate but has to be fought for. It largely depends upon the commander's ability to direct a battle in accordance with the change of events. One can change an unfavourable situation into a favourable one and passivity into initiative (e.g. the four-time crossing of the Cheshui River and the Battle of Jingzhou). Those who employ troops flexibly will usually have the initiative.

Choose a suitable commander who has creativity of thought and the ability to react speedily. There is neither a set form of employing troops nor an overall rule for winning a war. One has to blaze new trails constantly.

Attach importance to the creation of a brain trust which knows how to train staff officers as thinkers. They should not be used as copy clerks or orderlies. This is the only way in which a commander can pool the wisdom of his staff.

CHAPTER 6

Use of Spies

'Use of Spies' is the title of the last chapter of Sun Tzu's *The Art of War*. It points out the importance and the ways of using spies in a battle. The purpose of their use is to be aware of one's enemy. This develops Sun Tzu's idea: 'Knowing the enemy and oneself, one will be invincible.' Let us see how Sun Tzu explored this topic.

In the chapter on spies, Sun Tzu wrote: 'The reason the enlightened sovereign and the wise general often win the battle when they move, and their achievements surpass those of ordinary men, is foreknowledge. This foreknowledge cannot be elicited from spirits or gods, nor by analogy with experience, nor by astrologic calculations. It must be obtained from men who know the enemy's situation.

'In olden times, the rise of the Shang Dynasty was due to Yi Zhi, who had served under the Xia. The rise of the Zhou Dynasty was due to Lu Ya, who had served under the Yin. Therefore, only the enlightened sovereign and wise general who are able to use the most intelligent people as spies can achieve great results.

'Now there are five sorts of spies: native spies, internal spies, double spies, doomed spies, and surviving spies. When all these five types of spies are at work and their operations are clandestine, it is called the divine manipulation of threats and is the treasure of a sovereign.

'The sovereign must understand the activities of all five types of spies. He depends mainly on double spies for knowledge of the enemy situation, and therefore it is mandatory that they be treated with the utmost liberality. Hence, of all those in the army close to the commander, none is more intimate than the spies; of all rewards, none more liberal than those given to spies; of all matters, none is more confidential than those relating to spy operations.'

The most valuable aspect about Sun Tzu's *The Art of War* is that he worked out his strategies and tactics from actual war conditions and on the basis of full knowledge of the enemies. His idea of obtaining intelligence, or attaching importance to men who know the enemies' situation, is material. He used various means to collect information on an extensive scale. He was resolutely against the belief in spirits or gods, analogy with past events, and astrologic calculations applied to war strategies.

Sun Tzu wrote: 'Native spies are those from the enemy's country people whom we employ. Internal spies are enemy officials whom we employ. Double spies are enemy spies whom we employ. Doomed spies are those of our own spies who are deliberately given false information and told to report it to the enemy. Surviving spies are those who return from the enemy camp to report information.' Indeed, when these five types of spies are all at work, there is no respite for the enemy.

As for the scope of collecting information, Sun Tzu pointed out: 'In the case of armies you wish to strike, cities you wish to attack, and people you wish to assassinate, it is necessary to find out the names of the garrison officers, the aides-de-camp, the ushers, gatekeepers, and the bodyguards. Our spies must be instructed to ascertain these matters.' It goes without saying that the size of an enemy's area and the population and the storage of his materials are all within the scope of espionage.

The History of Spies

Those who have studied the history of Chinese and foreign wars are aware that the use of spies has been an important means of fighting a war. No doubt the ways of espionage have developed from primitive to complicated. Yet despite the highly technical age we live in, which enables us to use all modern devices including satellites, the use of spies still remains worthwhile for intelligence gathering between countries. The basic form of spying does not differ that much from what Sun Tzu summed up more than two thousand years ago. The following are examples of using native spies in ancient as well as modern times.

THE WAR BETWEEN CHU AND HAN During the war between the kingdoms of Chu and Han, an important official of the Chu army named Fan Zhen was well known for his resourcefulness and respected by Xiang Yu, the sovereign of Chu. Zhang Liang and Chen Ping, both counsellors in the court of Han, feared Fan Zhen because of his ability to see through schemes.

Chen Ping knew that Xiang Yu was very suspicious, so he thought of an excellent plan to use in their war. He sent a messenger with gifts and a fabricated letter to Fan Zhen to impersonate Fan Shi, Fan Zhen's nephew. In the letter, Fan Shi wrote that he was now an adviser under Liu Bong the sovereign of Han. He said Liu Bong was an open–minded and magnanimous ruler, so he was extremely happy serving him. The messenger specifically went to the Chu camp at a time when Fan Zhen was not there. He gave the letter and gifts to the sentry who thought it important to forward directly to Xiang Yu. Xiang Yu became suspicious after reading the letter. When Fan Zhen came back, Xiang asked him whether he had a nephew named Fan Shi. Fan Zhen confirmed this, but added that Fan Shi had died in his boyhood. Xiang Yu was then all the more suspicious that Fan Zhen had colluded with Liu Bong.

The next year, the representatives of Liu Bong and Xiang Yu started peace talks. When Xiang Yu's representative arrived in Han, Chen Ping pretended that he was expecting a representative from Fan Zhen rather than Xiang Yu. He had cancelled the rich feast which was supposed to have been given in honour of Fan Zhen's man. Instead, Chen Ping served Xiang Yu's representative with an ordinary dinner. When Xiang Yu heard about what happened in Han, his suspicions about Fan Zhen increased. Then he never listened to Fan's advice again. The relationship between them became strained day by day. Fan Zhen was forced to resign, and died on his way back to his home town. Until his last day he was unaware of the reason for Xiang Yu's change of attitude towards him. After that, Xiang Yu made all decisions on his own and courted defeat in the end. Chen Ping's scheme of driving a wedge between Xiang Yu and Fan Zhen succeeded.

During the period of the Three Kingdoms, Zhou Yu of the kingdom of Wu used the same kind of scheme which prompted Cao Cao to kill Cai Mao and Chang Yong, both of whom were his own admirals. As a result of this, Cao Cao was defeated in the Battle of Chibi.

HITLER'S FABRICATION OF SOVIET SPIES   On the eve of World War II, Hitler's intelligence officers fabricated information framing a case against General Tukhachevski, who was then a senior officer in the Soviet Red Army's Supreme Command. The information falsely accused him of working with Germany in an attempt to overthrow Stalin's leadership by force. A Soviet spy in Germany bought the information for a hundred thousand roubles. The Soviet Supreme Command was taken in, and not only was Tukhachevski shot, but a number of other Soviet generals were also implicated. This was one of the factors which accounted for the failure of the Soviet army in the beginning of the war against Nazi Germany.

Summary

Native and double spies are the most important types of spies to use against an enemy. Properly used, they can jeopardise the enemy's unity and disintegrate his forces. An enemy can also be disarmed by its own hand being caused to engage in internal strife.

Use of spies must be kept highly confidential. They must be extremely alert and resourceful; otherwise they are apt to be cheated, especially by double spies.

Spies must be liberally rewarded and their work highly appreciated. Spies must be boldly used. Their scope of activity and occupation must not be restricted. The only thing demanded of a spy is to fulfil the task for which he is entrusted.

CHAPTER 7

Geography

Of the thirteen chapters in Sun Tzu's *The Art of War* four chapters – 'The Nine Variables', 'Marches', 'Terrain' and 'The Nine Varieties of Ground' – deal with the relationships between geography and military affairs. In other chapters, there are also passages relating to geography.

The Importance of Terrain

The 'Terrain' chapter pointed out: 'Conformation of the ground is of great assistance in battle. Therefore, to estimate the enemy's attempts and to calculate the degree of difficulty and distances of the terrain in order to control forces of victory are tasks of a superior general. He who fights with full knowledge of these factors is certain to win, and he who does not is sure to be defeated.'

It must be made clear that what Sun Tzu meant by terrain is not the same term as used in a modern definition. It is rather a concept which has the implications of the modern 'topography' and 'military geography'.

Although Sun Tzu thought conformation of ground an assistance in battle, he asserted that a senior commander must be fully aware of the degree of difficulty and distances of terrain. Facts have proven his assertion. There have been numerous examples, abroad as well as in China, in which an army was defeated because of ignorance of terrain.

For example, in the year 645 BC, the kingdoms of Qin and Jin fought at Han Yuan [in present Shanxi Province]. The war chariots of Jin got stuck in the mire because the Jin commanders were ignorant of the terrain there. As a result, the Jin army was not only defeated, but Jinhuigong, the commander, was also captured.

In the year 589 BC, Qi kingdom was defeated by Jin. In re-treating, its chariots were entangled in a big clump of trees, almost resulting in the capture of its sovereign.

Sun Tzu, summing up numerous examples of this kind, ex-plained some of the effects that geography had on war. In the chapter entitled 'Terrain', he classified it in six types: 'accessible', 'entangling', 'temporising', 'narrow passes', 'precipitous' and 'dis-tant'. These types are terrains that are natural to a battlefield, and which fall generally into the category of topography.

In the chapter entitled 'Nine Varieties of Ground', he categ-orised ground as 'dispersive', 'frontier', 'key', 'open', 'focal', 'serious', 'difficult', 'encircled' and 'desperate'. These anticipated geographical situations which include strategic places beyond a boundary, and are generally related to military geography.

In his book, Sun Tzu discussed each category in detail and the ways to handle them. He gave much emphasis to fighting in a marsh or in a covered place. He pointed out: 'In crossing marshes, do it speedily. Do not linger in them. When on the march you find dangerous defiles or ponds covered with aquatic grasses, or hollow basins filed with reeds, or woods with dense tangled undergrowth, search them out carefully, for these are places where ambushes are laid and spies are hidden.'

This principle is still applicable in modern wars. In World War I, one hundred thousand Russian troops led by General Samsonov were completely annihilated by the German army in a marsh. And one can cite a number of examples in the modern history of war in which troops were intercepted and defeated at dangerous defiles and covered places.

Focal Ground

The importance of focal ground in connection with the present international situation – particularly the strategic deployments developed by the United States and the Soviet Union – is obvious and will be considered here.

Sun Tzu's definition of focal ground is: 'The area which is at the junction of three states is focal. He who gets control of it will gain the support of surrounding states . . . On focal ground, make allies of those states . . . And I would consolidate my alliances.'

Focal ground, generally speaking, is outside one's own territory, but it is strategically most important. If one occupies it first, one will be in a most favourable position. Apparently, since the focal ground is outside one's boundary, it can be far away. It is not easy to get control of it by mobilising one's troops. Therefore, Sun Tzu's means of taking control was to make allies of the states neighbouring the focal ground, which seems to be reasonable and feasible.

In the book *Sun Tzu's Art of War as Annotated by Eleven Authors* (Sung Edition), eight of the writers had the same explanation with regard to focal ground. They all believed that it is a strategically important place which has roads extended in all directions. It is vital, therefore, to have it under control first. The means to obtain it is, however, not by force but by diplomacy.

The following comment by Mr He is representative of the opinions of others: 'Focal ground is a junction which extends in all directions. Take hold of it first and the others will obey you. It gives security to get but is dangerous to lose.

'The sovereign of Wu once asked Sun Tzu: "If we are far off from the focal ground, we won't be able to reach it first even if we drive our horses and chariots as fast as possible. What shall I do?"

'Sun Tzu replied: "The distance is the same to us and to the enemy. To get control of the focal ground, we must attach more importance to wealth than force. If you reward your prospective allies with valuables and bind them with solemn covenants, you are there first even if your troops have not arrived. You are aided and your enemy is not." '

The meaning of his comments is clear. The main idea is to adopt diplomatic measures and economic means to win over the state in which the focal ground is situated.

The Rivalry Between the US and USSR

Sun Tzu's theory in this respect is of practical significance, which can be proven by examples of rivalry between the United States and the Soviet Union. Karl von Clausewitz often proved the correctness of his theoretical conclusions by giving examples from war history. He also attached great importance to topography, and once said that it is of special significance for the headquarters of the general staff to have knowledge of geography. And one can always find records of terrain in war history. Therefore, each headquarters of the general staff presently in various countries has set up a specific department to study geography.

According to the definition Sun Tzu gave to focal ground, and the annotations on it, there are quite a few strategically important places which can be said to be focal ground: the Strait of Gibraltar, the Suez Canal and the Strait of Bosphorus – the three passages in the Mediterranean Sea and the southern wing of NATO; the Strait of Malacca, between Indonesia and Malaysia; the Panama Canal in Central America; and the Persian Gulf and Gulf of Mexico – one in the east and one in the west.

As is known, one of the superpowers still finds it difficult to lay its hands on – but has not given up its attempt – the Strait of Gibraltar, which is firmly in the hands of the United Kingdom. But it has spent several billion dollars as military and economic 'aid' to Egypt in order to get the right of passage through the Suez Canal; it gave one billion dollars as 'aid' to Turkey, and its principal leader visited the country personally, to ensure its right of passage through the Strait of Bosphorus, which it succeeded in obtaining. The aircraft carrier SS *Kiev* secured a smooth passage through the Strait of Bosphorus into the Mediterranean, which was not permitted according to an international treaty. What this superpower did was in line with Sun Tzu's principle: 'One should attach enough importance to giving aid and send more envoys . . . '

The United States and the Soviet Union have been fighting for control of Afghanistan and several other countries around the Persian Gulf. The policy of Cuba, the focal ground east of the Gulf of Mexico, greatly changed the strategic position of the two superpowers in North and South America.

Tonga, a small country in the South Pacific, is at the strategic point among three allies: the United States, Australia and New Zealand. The Soviet Union tried a few years ago to cater to this country by 'giving economic aid and sending a number of envoys' in an attempt to get a foothold in the South Pacific. It did not succeed because its scheme was seen through.

Geography in the Space Age

The world has entered the space age, and various kinds of satellites have been widely used for military purposes, especially the space shuttle. All this has made it possible for a future war to be fought in space. But nothing can completely escape the confines of earth. Satellites and space shuttles alike are both launched from the ground, where the strategic points and economic bases are also located.

Therefore, geography is one of the four indispensable factors – in addition to the enemy's and one's own situations and the element of time – to be taken into consideration before making decisions and laying out plans. No doubt this is taught in all military academies in the world. When we study Sun Tzu's *The Art of War*, we should in no way neglect the practical significance of his doctrine with regard to geography.

Summary

Places of strategic importance include straits, canals, airports, gulfs or bays, and launching sites for guided missiles which are worthy of blockade and control. There are generally two ways of controlling them before the enemy does: one is to make an ally through diplomacy of the country where the place is situated; the other is to rent or lease the place through friendly negotiations so that it may not be used by the enemy.

Deserts, big marshes, forests, uninhabited areas, plagued regions, and high mountains where the air is thin are unfit places for a military troop to inhabit for long.

There are places one must fight for militarily. They include centres of communication or of military, political or economic importance. It is advantageous to occupy places where one can be the master of the situation, preserving the freedom to move troops. Places from which one can attack as well as retreat, where one can keep plentiful supplies, and where one can adapt to all kinds of changes, are all important.

Tactically valuable places generally are commanding heights above a battlefield, hubs of communication, solid and strong buildings on flatlands, bridgeheads and certain places for crossing along a river.

CHAPTER 8

Historical Background of Sun Tzu's
The Art of War

Mao Zedong wrote in an article: 'Where do correct ideas come from? Do they drop from the skies? No. Are they innate in the mind? No. They come from social practice, and from it alone. They come from three kinds of social practice: the struggle for production, the class struggle, and scientific experiment.'

Sun Tzu lived in the later Spring and Autumn Period, a time when ancient Chinese society was changing from a slave to a feudal society. This was the time when there was fierce class struggle reflected in wars. Prior to this period, five bo [a title of nobility in ancient China equivalent to an earl] – Qi Yuan, Jin Wen, Qin Mu, Chu Zhuang, and Song Rang – were fighting for dominance, and the whole social system was in turbulence.

According to historical records for the early Spring and Autumn Period, there had been more than 130 small states fighting against one another. In the process, there emerged five powerful states: Qi, Jin, Qin, Chu and Song (in fact, Song was not as strong as the others). They fought for overall control, bullying smaller and weaker states and invading their neighbours. During the period of about two hundred years before Sun Tzu lived, there had occurred three to four hundred wars among them. In addition to military struggles, which produced a diversified art of war, history had witnessed political struggles, economic struggles (reflected mainly in commercial relations and in the seizure of other states' wealth by economic practices), and diplomatic struggles (usually in alliances and counter-alliances, and protection of smaller states in order to enlarge one's sphere of influence). Sun Tzu's *The Art of War* was indeed a summary of the experiences of these wars. It is, therefore, still immortal two thousand years after it was written as far as many of its principles are concerned.

Sun Tzu's *The Art of War* seems to be speaking in abstract terms. But when we relate it to various wars that occurred before Sun Tzu, things become clearer. Of course, it is not the intention of the author to link each and every principle of Sun Tzu's *The Art of War* to an historic event. Only one or two examples are to be given to elaborate upon Sun Tzu's central ideas.

The Estimate of the Situation

'Estimates', the first chapter of Sun Tzu's *The Art of War*, appraises the role that preliminary calculations play in a war: 'If the calculations made in the temple before a battle indicate victory, it is because careful calculations show that your conditions for a battle are more favourable than those of your enemy; if they indicate defeat, it is because careful calculations show that favourable conditions for a battle are fewer. With more careful calculations, one can win, with less one cannot. How much less chance of victory has one who makes no calculations at all! By this means, one can foresee the outcome of a battle.'

The 'preliminary calculations' in modern times mean the decisions made by the highest command before a war after meticulous analysis regarding various factors of war. One does not enter a war if one is not sure to win. That is to say, the decision whether to enter a war is the outcome of a comprehensive study beforehand of various factors of political and military experience, and of diplomacy and geography. The following example should suffice to show what is meant by this.

THE WAR OF CHENG PU   The War of Cheng Pu in 632 BC was one of fairly large scale during the Spring and Autumn Period. It was also a war enabling Jin Wen Gong to secure his position of dominance and it laid the foundation for the Jin state to be supreme among states for a long time. Before the war, the monarch of Jin and his officials carefully weighed various factors pertaining to both sides. *Zou Zhuan,* a book about Chinese history, has a very vivid description of the war as follows: 'In winter, Chu and its followers besieged Sung. Gongsun Guru of Sung went to Jin for help.'

Xian Zhen, one of the marshals in Jin, said: 'This is the time for us to pay our debt of gratitude to Sung by coming to their rescue. It is also the time for us to obtain hegemony in the area.'

Hu Yen, a Jin general, also remarked: 'Chu secured the Cao state not long ago and it had matrimonial relations with the Wei state. If we attacked Cao and Wei, Chu would be sure to come to their rescue. Then Qi and Sung would certainly be relieved of Sung's siege.' Jin Wen Gong, the sovereign of Jin, followed their advice.

The next spring Jin's troops attacked Cao and Wei, and were victorious. But things turned out unexpectedly. Zi Yu, a senior general of Chu, continued its attack on the state of Sung, which again sent Man Yin to Jin to ask for emergency help.

During the discussion, Jin Wen Gong stated: 'If we do not try our best to help Sung, it will break off relations with us. If Chu is not in a mood of reconciliation, we shall have to go to war against it. In that case, it is essential to get help from Qi and Qin. But what if they decline?'

Xian Zhen replied; 'Tell Sung not to ask us but pay handsome tributes to Qi and Qin, and then ask them to plead with Chu. In the meantime, we, having kept the sovereign of Cao in captivity, will give a part of the territories of the Cao state and Wei state to Sung. Being closely allied with the two states, Chu will not tolerate it. Pleased with Sung's tributes and annoyed with Chu's stubbornness, Qi and Qin will certainly resort to arms with Chu.'

Subduing the Enemy Without a Fight

As we have already observed in Sun Tzu's *The Art of War*, there are such important principles as: 'to attack the enemy's strategy', 'to disrupt enemy's alliances', and 'to subdue the enemy without fighting'. That is to say, in fighting a war one must first attack the enemy's strategy and disrupt his diplomacy in order to subdue his troops without fighting.

Sun Tzu was against fighting a reckless war in the field with the enemy. He stressed: 'The next best is to attack the enemy's army, and the worst policy is to attack a walled city.' Both of these, he thought, should be done only when there is no alternative. This is really a wise remark of an experienced person in commanding battles. His conclusion was: 'To subdue the enemy's troops without fighting is the supreme excellence.'

Was this conclusion Sun Tzu's wishful thinking or was he just following his own inclinations? The answer is negative, because he came to this conclusion after summing up many war experiences in history.

Zou Zhuan recorded many outstanding military strategists who, with or without a powerful backup force, defeated a stronger enemy with the help of their wisdom, courage, insight and eloquence. They achieved the aim of subduing the enemy without fighting. There were two well-known wars before Sun Tzu's time which proved that principle.

THE BATTLE BETWEEN QI AND CHU   In 656 BC, Qi Huan Gong – allied with the states of Lu, Song, Chen, Wei, Zheng, Xu and Cao – attacked the powerful Chu state in the south. Facing aggressive troops from all sides, Chu was obviously inferior in numbers.

The emperor of Chu sent an envoy to Qi, asking Qi Huan Gong: 'You are in the north and we are in the south. We have nothing whatsoever to do with each other. What is the reason for your invading us, pray?'

Guan Zhong, a minister of the Qi state, instead of replying, brought the envoy to account for not paying tributes to Emperor Zhou (the common puppet monarch of all the states, in whose name Qi Huan Gong had launched the war against Chu). He also blamed Chu for the drowning of King Zhou Sao, which had already taken place a long time ago. The envoy of Chu admitted guilt in not paying tributes and promised to restore them soon, but denied any responsibility for King Zhou Sao's death. Qi was dissatisfied with the reply and continued its advance.

The sovereign of Chu sent another envoy, Qu Wan, to Qi to make further representations. While receiving the envoy, the sovereign of Qi purposefully asked his guards to create an impressive formation in an attempt to coerce Qu Wan into signing a treaty favourable to the state of Qi.

In a neither haughty nor humble manner, Qu Wan said: 'Who dares to disobey you if you placate various sovereigns with virtue and morals? But if you intend to use force, Mount Fangcheng would be our city wall and the Hanshui River our city moat [meaning that the city will be impregnable]. Even though you have a powerful army, it would be useless.'

This was diplomatic language used with perfect assurance. Qi

Huan Gong had to sign a peace treaty (not entirely favourable to Qi) with Chu and withdraw his troops. This example was significant in that Qi was powerful while Chu was gifted and just with its language. Both sides achieved their respective goals but the real winner was Chu.

PEACEFUL RELATIONS SUSTAINED WITH DIPLOMACY   In 579–546 BC, there was an anti-war movement launched by Hua Yuan and Xiang Shu, two militarists of the weak Sung state, which serves as a good example of subduing an enemy without fighting. At that time, smaller states like Zheng and Sung, sandwiched between the more powerful states of Jin and Chu, were often harassed by them. Zheng used to amass large numbers of slaves and jade and silk objects at the border, and give them as state gifts to whoever came to cause a skirmish. Sung suffered even more and in one siege by Chu, its subjects had to swap their children to be eaten as food.

The anti-war movement was launched under this circumstance and was successful. Sung persuaded all the neighbouring states (including Jin and Chu) to conclude a treaty with both Jin and Chu as leaders of the alliance.

The contents of the treaty included the provision: 'Jin and Chu shall not use force against each other. They shall be bound by a common cause and go through thick and thin together . . . Whoever breaks its pledge shall be struck dead by Heaven.'

The treaty also stipulated that the smaller states should pay tributes to Jin and Chu. Clearly, it was better for them to give out some money and valuables than to suffer from calamities of war. After the signing of this treaty, there emerged among the states a situation of tranquillity, particularly after the movement launched by Xiang Shu. For more than thirty years there was no major war between them.

The above-mentioned events were just as familiar to Sun Tzu as the wars of the past hundred years are to us. He had as much knowledge of the anti-war drive launched by Xiang Shu as we do of the history of the two world wars in the twentieth century. Therefore, his doctrine that 'the best way is to subdue an enemy without fighting' was based on historical fact.

Summary

As a whole, Sun Tzu attached great importance to employing politics, diplomacy and strategic considerations for the purpose of subduing an enemy. To some extent, this was a strategy based on one's economic strength. Obviously, Sun Tzu was of the opinion that one should make the enemy yield by means of one's powerful political and diplomatic capability and economic and military strength rather than by means of war. In today's language, this is called a 'policy backed up by strength', or strategy of nuclear deterrence. Sun Tzu was certainly the first person in world history to have put forward this doctrine. We can conclude that Sun Tzu's *The Art of War* was a product of experience gained during the Spring and Autumn Period. It was not fabricated out of imagination, nor was it copied from any conclusions of his predecessors.

CHAPTER 9

Naive Materialism and Primitive Dialectics

It is sometimes difficult correctly to appraise various occurrences in the world because of their differences in time, place, historical background, development, and end result. But it is often possible to prove the correctness of some relative truth from the success or failure of what has happened in accordance with the rule of historical development.

From a philosophical point of view, 'materialism is man's practical knowledge of the objective world which has been developed on the basis of his social practice.' It is praiseworthy for Sun Tzu to have written *The Art of War* by synthesising different social phenomena (mainly related to war) more than two thousand years ago, and learning from books on the art of war written by his predecessors.

Sun Tzu's *The Art of War* brings to light many common laws of war, discusses rather comprehensively factors leading to victory in a war, and reflects the thought of naive materialism and primitive dialectics.

During the Spring and Autumn Period, China was going through the transitional stage from slave society to feudal society. In the duration of its five hundred years, different schools of thought – developed by Confucius, Mencius, Yangzi, Mozi, Zhuangzi, Laozi and Sun Tzu – spread widely. With the development of society, some of them died out, but some continued to spread. Sun Tzu's doctrine is among those which has been popular since then. This fully demonstrates its practical value.

Sun Tzu's *The Art of War* contains thoughts of naive materialism and primitive dialectics that are reflected in many of his statements. The following are some of the obvious ones: 'Thus, the reason the enlightened ruler and the wise general conquer the enemy whenever they strike and their achievements surpass those of ordinary men is foreknowledge. This foreknowledge cannot be elicited from spirits, nor from gods, nor by analogy with past events, nor from deductive calculations. It must be obtained from men who know the enemy situation.' Sun Tzu did not believe in gods, spirits or divination; nor did he rely upon astrology for his actions. It is the pride of our national culture that Sun Tzu was an atheist even more than two thousand years ago.

Atheism vs. Theism

There has been long rivalry between the two world outlooks – atheism and theism – and that has obviously been reflected in military affairs. We know from inscriptions on bones and tortoise shells of the Shang Dynasty and on bronze objects that in ancient times divination was frequently practised in China before fighting to forecast the result of war.

In ancient times, there were debates between generals with materialist ideas and those who were superstitious over whether or not it was favourable to move troops on the day of Jiazi. The argument the former gave in refutation of the latter was that the Battle of Muye (1098 BC) was launched on the day of Jiazi. It was a victory for the King Zhou Wu and disaster for King Ying Zhou. This was a powerful argument.

In spite of the fact that Sun Tzu refuted superstitions, there still have been quite a few fatuous generals and commanders who practised divination before moving troops. That has been so not only in China, but also in the West. About half a century before the Christian era, the Roman Julius Caesar was having a war with the Germanic people. In one of the battles, only half of the main force of the Germanic army was fighting. This resulted in a big victory for the Roman army, which would have surely been defeated if its enemy's main force had joined the fight. According to a statement made by a Germanic prisoner of war, the reason that the Germanic main force did not join the fight was because its leaders believed that the gods did not wish the Germanic army to fight before the crescent moon rose, or else they would suffer defeat.

All this illustrates how commendable Tzu's materialistic thought of atheism was. His principle that 'must be obtained from men who know the enemy situation' did not apply only to the use of spies. In fact, his emphasis upon the role of men was reflected in his exposition of political, diplomatic and economic factors that bore upon a war. His materialistic doctrines reflected that the ruler should have 'the people in harmony with them' and 'calculations in temple'. The enemy's strategies and alliances should be disrupted. 'After one thousand pieces of gold are in hand, one hundred thousand troops may be raised.'

Sun Tzu's Primitive Dialectical Thought

There are also many statements in Sun Tzu's *The Art of War* that reflect his primitive dialectical thought. We can easily pick out some of his remarks that are in accord with the law of the unity of opposites. For example: extraordinary and normal, void and actuality, circuitous and straight, strong and weak, victorious and defeated, favourable and unfavourable, enemy and oneself, numerous and scanty, fatigued and at ease, well fed and hungry, turbulence and peace, noisy and quiet, advance and retreat, far and near, gain and loss, and brave and cowardly.

While expounding void and actuality, he held that there must be void in actuality and vice versa. In the chapter entitled 'Posture of Army', he wrote: 'In battle there are only the normal and extraordinary forces, but their combinations are limitless; none can comprehend them all.' And he added: 'To ensure your army will sustain the enemy's attack without suffering defeat is a matter of operating the extraordinary and the normal forces . . . For these two forces are mutually reproductive; their interaction as endless as that of interlocked rings. Who can determine where one ends and the other begins?'

He strongly maintained that one must consider both favourable and unfavourable factors while making judgments. He pointed out in the chapter entitled 'The Nine Variables': 'The wise general in his deliberations must consider both favourable and unfavourable factors. By taking into account the favourable factors, he makes his plan feasible; by taking into account the unfavourable, he may resolve the difficulties.'

He again pointed out in the chapter 'Manoeuvring': 'Those skilled in war avoid the enemy when its spirit is keen, and attack it when it is sluggish and the soldiers are homesick. This is control of the moral factor. In good order, they await an enemy in disorder; in serenity, an enemy in clamorousness. This is control of the mental factor. Close to the field of battle, they await an enemy coming from afar; at rest, they await an exhausted enemy; with well-fed troops, they await a hungry enemy. This is control of the physical factor. They do not engage an enemy advancing with well-ordered banners, nor one whose formations are in impressive array. This is control of the factor of changing circumstances.'

From the above-mentioned doctrines of Sun Tzu, it can be seen that he was full of dialectical ideas in line with the universal law of unity of opposites.

In exploring Sun Tzu's theories, we also find that his thinking was systematic and objective. Judging from the way in which he looked at the nature and law of the world, his logical thinking was quite rigorous and, therefore, worthy of esteem.

CHAPTER 10

Universal Laws of War

Sun Tzu pointed out in the chapter entitled 'Use of Spies': 'Thus, the reason the enlightened ruler and the wise general conquer the enemy whenever they strike is foreknowledge.' Foreknowledge, in essence, means to know the situation of the enemy and of yourself before the war starts, just as Sun Tzu wrote in the chapter entitled 'Offensive Strategy': 'Know the enemy and know yourself; in a hundred battles you will never be defeated. When you are ignorant of the enemy but know yourself, your chances of winning or losing are equal. If ignorant both of the enemy and of yourself, you are sure to be defeated in every battle.' No commanders – whether in modern or ancient times, in China or abroad – can afford to ignore this principle.

It is a universal law which is without parallel in history, and it represents the best of Sun Tzu's thought. Philosophically, it belongs to naive materialism. From the point of view of war theory, it is a fundamental law of making judgment and analysis. And from the viewpoint of directing a war, it constitutes an important choice of first looking for conditions that may lead to victory and then for opportunities that would lead to a sure victory.

Modern Intelligence Gathering

Today, the funds that the Soviet Union and the United States spend on intelligence gathering for the purpose of knowing each other's dealings are terrific. One United States general who had been in charge of intelligence work pointed out that since the end of World War II, the US had spent no less than $50 to $75 billion on the establishment of an intelligence system. He added that in spite of this, the US was in no better a position than it was before the invasion of Pearl Harbor in 1941. This statement was made in the 1970s. Today one can well imagine how high the intelligence expenses are. As for the Soviet Union, it keeps its defence expenses top secret, but it is not difficult to infer how much money it spends on its intelligence work.

Mao Zedong highly appreciated Sun Tzu's principle, saying that it remains a scientific truth today. In addition, he pointed out in his essay 'Problems of Strategy in China's Revolutionary War': 'Some people are good at knowing themselves and poor at knowing their enemy, and some are the other way around; neither can solve the problem of learning and applying the laws of war. There is a saying in the book of Sun Tzu, the great military scientist of ancient China, "Know the enemy and know yourself, and in a hundred battles you will never be defeated", which refers both to the stage of learning and to the stage of application, both to knowing the laws of the development of objective reality and to deciding on our own action in accordance with these laws in order to overcome the enemy facing us. We should not take this saying lightly.'

Let us examine the theoretical principles of practical significance in *The Art of War* from three aspects – political, economic, and the art of direction.

The Political Aspect

Quite a few problems Sun Tzu discussed about war fall within the political aspect. For example, he said: 'War is a matter of vital importance to the state; a matter of life or death; the road either to survival or to ruin. Hence, it is imperative that it be studied thoroughly. Therefore, appraise it in terms of the five fundamental factors and make comparisons of various conditions of the enemy and yourself when seeking the outcome of war. The first of the fundamental factors is politics; the second, weather; the third, terrain; the fourth, the commander; and the fifth, doctrine.' 'What is of supreme importance in war is to attack the enemy's strategy; next best is to disrupt the enemy's alliances.'

Most of these statements involve political activities before or during a war. All these doctrines had never been and could never be put forward systematically before Sun Tzu's time. He systematically brought military actions into political scope. By politics, he meant the ways to cause the people to be in harmony with their ruler. That is to say, the ruler has to impose his will upon the people and only in so doing can he succeed in making the people accompany him in war and peace without fear of mortal peril. In other words, only when political harmony is achieved can it be possible to defeat the enemy. By the commander, he meant the ability and qualities which a commander should have. And by doctrine, he meant the military organisation, system and regulations. In short, three of the five factors are directly connected with politics. Among the seven elements he mentioned, the first, second, fourth, fifth and seventh are directly related to politics – namely, which ruler is wiser and more able, which commander is the more talented, in which army regulations and instructions are better carried out, which troops are the stronger, and which side administers rewards and punishments in a more enlightened manner.

Sun Tzu was one of the first persons in ancient China who believed that diplomacy was one of the keys to the outcome of war. In military works before Sun Tzu, there had been similar discussions about the importance of diplomacy, but none had summarised it into theory as Sun Tzu did.

Sun Tzu discussed the relationships between war and politics, and from there he proceeded to the gravity, cruelty and disruptive-ness of war. He pointed out: 'When the army engages in protracted campaigns, the resources of the state will fall short. When your weapons are dulled and ardour dampened, your strength exhausted and treasure spent, the chieftains of neighbouring states will take advantage of your crisis to act. In that case, no man, however wise, will be able to avert the disastrous consequences that ensue.'

It is true that Sun Tzu was not able to formulate the scientific principles: 'War is the continuation of politics', 'Politics is war without bleeding', or 'War is politics with bleeding', but he was clearly aware that whether you will be victorious or defeated, much depends upon whether your government is honest and upright and your system is good. He wrote as a conclusion in the chapter 'Dispositions': 'Those skilled in war cultivate politics, preserve the laws and institutions, and are therefore able to formu-late victorious policies.' It is commendable for Sun Tzu as a military commander to have been aware of the important effect that politics has on war.

Karl von Clausewitz stated: 'War is the continuation of politics.' This well-known dictum has been understood in the West to be an insightful remark. Now it has been found that a similar remark was made in an ancient Chinese writing, *The Strategy of Warring States,* as early as the Qin Dynasty. It explicitly stated: 'It is impossible to gain profit without making efforts and to extend one's territory by sitting idly. Even the five emperors and three kings could not achieve that. The only way to attain that goal is to continue doing it through war.' Obviously, gaining profits and extending one's territory are all political aims. One has to achieve that through war.

In *The Art of War,* written by Sun Bin, excavated from the Yin Que Mountains, it is recorded: 'It is impossible for a sovereign whose prestige and ability are not comparable to the five emperors and three kings to carry out a policy of humanity, justice and virtue, and be a model of civility. This was, in fact, yearned for by Yao and Shun [legendary monarchs and sages in ancient China], but found to be impossible. One had to solve certain problems by force.' This is tantamount to achieving a political aim through war.

The Economic Aspect

Before we discuss Sun Tzu's idea concerning the effects of economics upon war, it is necessary for us to quote relevant passages from *Guan Zi,* a book published one century earlier than Sun Tzu's, which reflects Guan Zhong's thought on military economics, in order to have a better understanding of military theories in ancient China.

In the book *Guan Zi,* it is written: 'If the state is wealthy, it will not be short of supplies even if the war lasts long; if the state has excellent weapons, it will not be exhausted after repeated attacks. If the army has any important matter, it is weapons. If it is not well equipped, you are giving away your troops for nothing. If you fight for one year, ten years' accumulation will be exhausted. An all-out war will exhaust all you have.' All this means that it is difficult to fight a war without ample funds and excellent weapons.

Sun Tzu also attached great importance to relations between military actions and economics. He wrote: 'In operations of war – when one thousand fast four-horse chariots, one thousand heavy chariots, and one thousand mail-clad soldiers are required; when provisions are transported for a thousand *li;* when there are expenditures at home and at the front and stipends for entertainment of envoys and advisers – the cost of materials such as glue and lacquer, and of chariots and armour, will amount to one thousand pieces of gold a day. One hundred thousand troops may be dispatched only when this money is in hand . . . If you fight with such a big army, a speedy victory is required. If victory is long delayed, troops will be exhausted and morale depressed. When troops attack cities, their strength will be exhausted.'

He added: 'Those skilled in war do not require a second levy nor more than two provisions. They carry military equipment from the homeland, but rely on the enemy for provisions. Thus, the army is plentifully provided with food.'

'When a country is impoverished by military operations, it is because of distant transportation; carrying supplies for great distances renders the people destitute. Where troops are gathered, prices go up. When prices rise, the wealth of the people is drained away. When wealth is drained away, the peasantry will be afflicted with urgent exactions. With this loss of wealth and exhaustion of strength, the households in the central plains will be extremely poor and seven-tenths of their wealth dissipated. As to government expenditures, those due to broken-down chariots, worn-out horses, armour and helmets, bows and arrows, spears and shields, protective mantlets, draft oxen and wagons will amount to 60 per cent of the total.'

It is clear that Sun Tzu set great store by economics, namely the financial situation of a country. His principle of fighting a speedy battle to force a quick decision originated from this idea. He believed that prolonged war was something that exhausted the wealth of a country. If financial resources dried up, additional taxes would be levied on people; as a result, the homes of the people would be stripped bare. This vicious cycle would lead to attacks from neighbouring states. In this case: 'No man, however wise, will be able to avert the consequences that ensue.'

Sun Tzu was quite practical and realistic. While discussing relationships between war and economics, he emphasised the use of resources and manpower of the enemy state. He wrote: 'One *zhong* [a measurement in ancient China] of the enemy's provisions is equivalent to twenty of one's own; one *shi* [approximately 60 kilograms] of the enemy's fodder to twenty *shi* of one's own.' He strongly maintained that one should offer big rewards to one's soldiers and treat captives well. One should utilise the captured weapons, military materials and prisoners of war to replenish one's own troops in order to support the war. These ideas of his were progressive ones of the new emerging feudal class.

During the war of liberation in China, several millions of Jiang Jieshi troops were captured by the PLA and became its staunch fighters after political education. As for the amount of weapons captured from the enemy, including tanks, cannons, warships and airplanes, it was unprecedented at home and abroad. This he called 'winning a battle and becoming stronger'.

Compared with wars in ancient times, the dependence of modern wars on economics is far greater. Even the powerful and financially secure United States felt it difficult to cope with a protracted war in Vietnam. General Westmoreland, the American commander in chief in Vietnam, quoted Sun Tzu as his argument for withdrawing his troops: 'There has never been a protracted war from which a country has benefited.'

Therefore, it is clear that the more modernised an army is, the more dependent it is on economics. Sun Tzu's doctrine about relationships between war and economics has not lost its significance with the passage of time.

The Art of Direction

We have discussed problems of war from the strategic point of view in previous chapters. In this section, we will approach it from the tactical side – in other words, from the aspect of the art of directing a war. (Sun Tzu made no clear distinction between strategy and direction in his thirteen chapters.) Discussion about the art of direction appeared in several chapters in Sun Tzu's *The Art of War*. However, here we will limit it to two aspects: initiative and flexibility.

INITIATIVE   How does one have the initiative? This is the primary question to answer while discussing the art of direction. If you lose the initiative in the battlefield, you will be thrown into passivity and be attacked at all times. Sun Tzu's idea of maintaining the initiative was primarily reflected in his doctrines 'to bring the enemy to the battlefield and not be brought there by him' and 'a victorious army tries to create conditions for victory before seeking battle'. All wise generals should try their best to utilise these ideas.

Sun Tzu advocated: 'A skilful commander takes up a position in which he cannot be defeated and seizes every opportunity to win over his enemy. Thus, a victorious army tries to create conditions for victory before seeking battle; an army destined to be defeated fights in the hope of gaining victory by sheer luck.' 'Generally, he who comes to the battlefield first and awaits his enemy is at ease; he who comes later and rushes into the fight is weary. And therefore, those skilled in war bring the enemy to the field of battle and are not brought there by him.'

It is a truth that one should try to impose one's will on the enemy. And only when you take up a position in which you cannot be defeated – in other words, you have the initiative in hand – can you take measures to move enemy troops and lead them to defeat.

When you first occupy a favourable position in the battlefield you can move enemy troops and transform the conditions between the enemy and yourself, just as Sun Tzu advised. All military scientists, ancient or contemporary, Chinese or foreign, know that war is a contest of strength, and strength can be transformed. When the sides are evenly matched (or even if the enemy is stronger), if we have the initiative, the situation can be transformed. If we are able to tire the enemy who is at ease, we .shall succeed in obtaining a favourable situation in which we can await the enemy.

THE RUSSIAN–JAPANESE WAR   Early in the twentieth century, the Baltic fleet of Tsarist Russia was totally annihilated during the Russian-Japanese War. The victory was achieved – according to Marshal Togo Heihachiro the Japanese commander in this sea battle – due to the application of Sun Tzu's doctrine 'to wait at one's ease for an exhausted enemy'. It was true that Russia's Baltic fleet committed a disastrous mistake by sailing all the way to the Far East, exhausting its sailors, while the Japanese navy was waiting for them at its ease.

The Baltic Sea was tens of thousands of kilometres away from the Sea of Japan. Furthermore, the Russian fleet was not in a position to reach the Far East by passing through the British-controlled Strait of Gibraltar, and then going through the Mediterranean Sea and the Suez Canal, because Britain was an ally of Japan. It had to go around the Cape of Good Hope, an additional voyage of over ten thousand kilometres.

In addition, after the Baltic fleet crossed the Malacca Strait, the

Japanese army spread false information (in accordance with Sun Tzu's doctrine, 'War is based on deception') to the effect that the Japanese navy was ready to launch a surprise attack upon the Tsarist fleet in the South China Sea. Being taken in, the Baltic fleet had to sail all the time in combat readiness, which added to its weariness, and the seamen were totally exhausted when they reached the Tsushima Strait. The Japanese navy had been waiting at ease and therefore, won an unprecedented victory over the Russian fleet.

FLEXIBILTY   Moving troops flexibly is another important principle in Sun Tzu's *The Art of War*. He advocated: 'Just as water has no constant shape, there are in warfare no constant conditions. Thus, one able to win victory by modifying his tactics in accordance with the enemy situation may be said to be divine.' He added that moving troops should be like the snakes of Mount Chang which respond simultaneously: 'When struck on the head, its tail attacks; when struck on the tail, its head attacks; when struck in the centre, both head and tail attack.'

In short, he maintained that one should adapt to the enemy's situation, and he opposed rigid tactics and mechanical materialism in war. He was also opposed to using outmoded methods. He was in favour of using normal and extraordinary forces, the solid and the void, the true and the false interchangeably, in order to confuse the enemy and obtain victory.

For the sake of carrying out his own propositions, Sun Tzu often tried to occupy a position of initiative and take pre-emptive measures. He pointed out: 'Speed is the essence of war. Take advantage of the enemy's unpreparedness, make your way by unexpected routes, and attack the enemy where he is unguarded.' It was because of these flexible tactics that he could keep the enemy units from uniting, cooperating, and supporting each other.

A commander should be very clear about the field situation and learn an art of direction with which he can manipulate the enemy. Sun Tzu wrote: One who is skilled at making the enemy move does so by creating a situation according to which the enemy will act; he entices the enemy with something he is certain to take. He keeps the enemy on the move by holding out bait, and then attacks him with picked troops.'

With regard to manipulating the enemy, there is an incisive

statement in the chapter entitled 'Void and Actuality': 'Analyse the enemy's plans so that you will know his shortcomings as well as strong points. Agitate him in order to ascertain the pattern of his movement. Lure him out to reveal his dispositions and ascertain his position. Launch a probing attack in order to learn where his strength is abundant and where deficient.' In this way, he can achieve what Sun Tzu said: 'His offensive will be irresistible if he makes for his enemy's weak positions; he cannot be overtaken when he withdraws, if he moves swiftly . . . When I wish to give battle, my enemy, even though protected by high walls and deep moats, cannot help but engage me, for I attack a position he must relieve. When I wish to avoid fighting, I may defend myself simply by drawing a line on the ground; the enemy will be unable to attack me because I divert him from going where he wishes.'

If you can move as flexibly as Sun Tzu described, you can certainly dominate the battlefield. 'Thus, I say that victory can be achieved. For even if the enemy is numerically stronger, I can prevent him from engaging.'

The essence of using troops flexibly is the principle: 'War is based on deception.' It is stated in the chapter entitled 'Estimates': 'All warfare is based on deception. Therefore, when capable of attacking, feign incapacity; when active in moving troops, feign inactivity; when near the enemy, make it appear that you are far away; when far away, make it seem that you are near.' It all shows flexibility to be capable or incapable, active or inactive, far away or near. For instance, the principle that 'when far away, make it seem that you are near' means that you should try to manoeuvre near the enemy in order to confuse him, when you are actually moving troops at a place far away.

The following are two examples showing two famous generals' (one ancient and the other contemporary) success in using this principle.

HAN'S CAMPAIGN AGAINST CHU   In 205 BC, Han Xin (of the Han state) wanted to attack Wei Wangbao (of the Chu state) across the Yellow River. Han's intention was to attack Wei from the rear at Anyi [in the present Anyi County, Shanxi Province], from faraway Xiayang [n the present Hanchen, Shan Xi Province]. But he created a diversion by collecting materials for crossing the

Yellow River at a nearby place called Linjing, as if he planned to cross the river there. Wei Wangbao was taken in by the action and deployed his main force along Linjing, and Anyi was left unguarded. Consequently, Han Xin's troops crossed the river at Xiayang without resistance. This was one of the main campaigns between the Chu and Han states.

THE INVASION OF NORMANDY In the European landing operation during World War II, US General Eisenhower decided that the Allied forces should land at Normandy in the northwest of France. But he hinted that the troops were going to land at the Calais area by the visible movement of army, navy and air forces, and by establishing a headquarters in that area. Eisenhower also had false information spread and a sham telegram sent in order to confuse Hitler. As a result, Nazi Germany was fooled and concentrated its main force along the Calais area. Finally, the Allied forces landed at Normandy successfully.

MAO ZEDONG'S EMPHASIS ON INITIATIVE AND FLEXIBILITY
In his military writings, Mao Zedong also stressed the important role that initiative and flexibility play in a war. He compared initiative to an army's freedom of action: 'Freedom of action is the very life of an army and once it is lost, the army is close to defeat or destruction.' He also made brilliant observations on flexibility: 'Flexibility consists in the intelligent commander's ability to take timely and appropriate measures on the basis of objective conditions after "judging the hour and sizing up the situation" (including the enemy's situation, our situation and the terrain), and this flexibility is "ingenuity in varying tactics".'

It is entirely practical to examine Sun Tzu's theory with this yardstick. There is a large amount of practical theory discussed with regard to the art of direction in Sun Tzu's The Art of War. Only notable ideas have been discussed in this writing.

CHAPTER 11

Obsolete Ideas in Sun Tzu's The Art of War

Truth develops constantly with the progress of times. Mao Zedong pointed out in his writing *On Practice*: 'The movement of change in the world of objective reality is never-ending, and so is man's cognition of truth through practice.' Keeping this in mind while evaluating Sun Tzu's *The Art of War*, a correct conclusion can be reached.

Generally speaking, when ancient academic works are assessed, it is not wrong to affirm or negate something by saying: 'Because of limitations of times and class . . . ' But it seems to provide the readers with a deeper understanding of the ancient work if it is appraised with an eye to the background in which it was written.

The main shortcomings of Sun Tzu's *The Art of War* are that it does not discuss the nature of war. According to the statistics gathered by historians, there occurred approximately four to five hundred big or small wars during the Spring and Autumn Period when Sun Tzu lived. Mencius, a famous scholar who lived some time later than Sun Tzu, made a widely acknowledged conclusion: 'There were no just wars during the Spring and Autumn Period.' Is this conclusion correct? The answer is negative.

The wars between the big powers during that period were definitely unjust, but those launched by smaller nations against the aggression of big powers were quite another matter. For instance, Sung, a small state, was besieged by two big powers, Jin and Chu, and its people had to exchange their children with one another to be eaten as food. Was not Sung on the just side when it fought against the aggressors?

In the history book *Zou Zhuan*, there were accounts of many uprisings by serfs from the seventh to sixth century BC. Famous among them were the insurrection of serfs in Qi against the construction of city walls, and the rebellion of serfs in Zhen against the ruling class. Were the serfs not on the just side when they rose against oppression of the ruling class and the serf owners as a result of intensification of class contradictions? Unfortunately, this is not considered in Sun Tzu's *The Art of War*. This could not but be regarded as an outstanding shortcoming and a policy of keeping the soldiers in ignorance.

This obscurantist policy was a flaw in Sun Tzu's work. No doubt he wrote: 'Regard your soldiers as your children', and 'Command them with civility but keep them under control by iron discipline.' It seems that he was propagating concern for soldiers and attention to discipline in the army. But what he did during the war was quite the opposite. He went so far as to maintain that the commander 'should be capable of keeping his officers and men in ignorance of his plans . . . He drives his men now in one direction, now in another, like a shepherd driving a flock of sheep, and none knows where he is going . . . The business of a general is to kick away the ladder behind soldiers when they have climbed up a height.' All these can be said to be reactionary ideas of looking down upon the labouring people.

The second shortcoming is that he overemphasised the function of generals. He stated: 'The general who understands how to employ troops is the minister of the people's fate and arbiter of the nation's destiny.' Related to this was another view of his: 'There are occasions when the commands of the sovereign need not be obeyed.' There have been quite a few generals who, affected by this view, used it as a pretext for not obeying orders from the supreme command. Is this view correct? Since there has been war by mankind, it has always been conditioned by politics, and has never and in no way departed from politics. Therefore, it often causes irremediable damage to the nation if long-term and overall interests of the state are given up for the sake of local interests in the battlefield.

It is argued that in ancient times communications were poor and difficult and situations at the front changed quickly, so commanders had to act arbitrarily in order to cope with the changing situation. Tenable as the argument might be, the situation today has greatly changed. Nowadays, with the help of telecommunication, television and man-made satellites, the supreme command has every small change in the battlefield at its fingertips. It is, therefore, entirely in a position to readjust its deployment or tactics in accordance with the new situation. A commander is in no way allowed to disobey orders from the supreme command for local interest. As a common rule of war, Sun Tzu's principle 'there are occasions when the commands of the sovereign need not be obeyed' is now obsolete.

Sun Tzu's Contradictions

The third point is that some of his principles are too rigid and mechanical. For example: 'Do not thwart an army which is returning homewards. One must leave a way of escape to a surrounded enemy, and do not press a desperate enemy too hard.' These principles are contradictory to many others in Sun Tzu's *The Art of War* itself. For instance, consider his advice to ' . . . avoid the enemy when its spirit is keen and attack it when it is sluggish and the soldiers are homesick'. It is just the opposite of the former ones mentioned. The latter principle is, without a shadow of doubt, the correct one.

Sun Tzu suggested in the chapter entitled 'Offensive Strategy' to surround an enemy when you are ten to his one. This is the idea of the 'war of annihilation', which is certainly correct. Of course, you should not leave a way of escape to the enemy if you surround him. During the Huai-Hai campaign, if the PLA had left an outlet for the enemy to flee, it would have been as if it let the tiger return to the mountains. In that case, how could the PLA have achieved the victory of totally wiping out the enemy force? The view that 'one must leave a way of escape to a surrounded enemy' is considered too rigid because of the word 'must.' It can also be feasible or even advantageous to leave an outlet free for the enemy in case one wants to wind up the campaign speedily or to lure the enemy to fall into an ambush.

As for the doctrine to 'not press a desperate enemy too hard', it is simply ludicrous. Mao Zedong had two very famous verses in one of his poems, which read:

> With power and to spare we must pursue the tottering foe,
> And not ape Xiang Yu the Conqueror seeking idle fame.

Sun Tzu's *The Art of War* is a military work written more than two thousand years ago. However, many of its doctrines, principles and rules are still of practical and universal significance. Therefore, it remains a valuable asset for the Chinese people and will remain so in any future war against aggression.

In spite of all this, the book, which was written in the interest of the emerging feudalistic class, inevitably has some backward or even reactionary views, owing to the limitations of the times and the author's class status. These shortcomings should be kept in perspective in the course of research. In this way, military science can be developed and new ideas brought forth.

THE BOOK OF LORD SHANG

THE BOOK OF LORD SHANG
CONTENTS

INTRODUCTION

From a text whose subject is warfare we turn now to a text of political theory in which warfare is regarded as one of the principal activities of the state and in which *The Art of War* is referred to as an authority. *The Book of Lord Shang* (*Shang chun shu* [*Shang jun shu*]) is one of the major surviving classics of the ancient Chinese school of philosophy known as Legalism or the School of Law (*fa chia* [*fa jia*]). Legalism developed during the fourth and third centuries BC in direct response to the political conditions of the time, and it is best to begin our approach to this text by looking again at this important historical background, this time with slightly different emphases.

Like the views put forward in Sun Tzu's *The Art of War*, Legalism was conceived and developed during the time in Chinese history aptly called the Period of the Warring States, 403–221 BC. As we have seen already, during this time China as the unified state we now know did not exist. The territory which was eventually to become China was divided into a number of autonomous smaller states constantly vying with each other for political advantage. The history of the period is one of alliance, counter-alliance, treaties made and broken, and above all, warfare. In the course of the fourth century BC alone some seven feudal lords each took the title of king, and even the pretence of loyalty to the emperor was dropped. What was chronically missing was political stability. As urgent as the question of how to win in battle was that of how to gain real political power and – no less important – how to sustain it. This issue exercised rulers and philosophers alike.

Before the Warring States Period, the organisation of Chinese society in its several states was feudal. Each state was divided into small domains ruled by a hereditary nobility. There was nothing we would recognise as a written legal code in these domains: rather, the nobles ruled in accordance with customs (*li*) handed down over the generations, and the peasantry – who lived in a condition of serfdom – simply did as they were bidden by their lord. These customs would undoubtedly serve the interests of the ruling families, who would, moreover, consider themselves exempt from subjection to them. In summary, then, the form of society which had failed to bring stability and which began to crumble during the time of the Warring States was feudal, and one in which there were many loci of power and influence (the noble families) within each state. There was nothing approximating to a written code of laws valid across a whole state and for all classes within the state. Bearing this in mind will make clear, as we go along, how daring and revolutionary was the political doctrine formulated by the Legalists.

Shang Yang (also sometimes referred to by his family name Kung-sun Yang), the putative author of the present text, was born into this political climate, probably in the first half of the fourth century BC. Manifestly a political thinker of considerable penetration and a man of great personal ambition and dynamism (not to say ruthlessness), Shang believed he knew how to solve the central political problems of his time, and he set about doing so with great single-mindedness, as is made clear in his life story, related in ch. 68 of Ssu-ma Ch'ien's [Sima Qian's] *Historical Records* (Shih chi [Shiji] first century BC). Shang Yang was a native of the state of Wei. An able and ambitious young scholar, he gained a minor post under a minister in Wei but failed to gain the approval of the ruling duke. As his patron the minister lay dying, he is said to have implored the Duke of Wei either to promote Shang or to execute him at once, so much did he fear what Shang would be like if he were to use his talents in the service of a state other than Wei. The duke did neither – a judgment he was to rue – and Shang, hungry for real power, took his ideas to the state of Ch'in [Qin]. There by astute behaviour he gained the favour of Duke Hsiao [Xiao] (ruled 361–338 BC). Shang convinced the Duke that the way to consolidate his power and to make Ch'in victorious over its rivals was to adopt the Legalist programme Shang put forward, and he was given the power to do this.

As will be seen in more detail presently, the central plank of this programme is the institution of a corpus of law which is applied absolutely uniformly and without exception to all the citizens of the state. Such was Shang's power that when the Crown Prince of Ch'in broke the new laws, punishment was meted out to him, albeit in his case not directly. On this occasion, Shang had to be content with punishing the prince's tutor, as the person responsible for forming his character. Shang had no difficulty in convincing Duke Hsiao that it would be greatly to the territorial advantage of Ch'in to destroy Wei (the state which had failed to recognise Shang's talent), and he was put in charge of the invasion forces. Personally acquainted with the Wei prince in command of the enemy forces, Shang tricked him into a parley, seized him and annihilated the Wei army (341 BC). As a result, much of the territory of Wei was ceded to Ch'in and on his return, Shang was rewarded with land and with ennoblement as Lord Shang.

However, like all who rise to power at the expense of others, Shang had made many enemies, and he had not been wise enough, despite having been well counselled to do so, to moderate the brutality of his policies when their major objectives had been gained. As another major figure in the Legalist school, Han Fei (b. around 280 BC) records, so much hated was he that 'when he came and went at court, [Lord Shang] was guarded by iron spears and heavy shields to prevent sudden attack' (*Han Fei Tzu* [*Hanfeizi*], section 18. Burton Watson's version p.94) His personal position was seriously flawed, in that his power depended entirely on the protection of Duke Hsiao. When the duke died in 338 BC he was succeeded by the Crown Prince whom Shang had punished and mortally offended. Once this happened, his numerous enemies among the nobles of Ch'in were not long in forming a conspiracy to bring him down. Ch'in troops were soon sent after him, and defeated Shang and his retainers in battle. Shang was killed and his body torn to pieces by chariots. His family was exterminated (338 BC).

It is not at all likely that Shang Yang was the historical author of the text which bears his name, though it is more than possible that the parts of the text composed first do reflect his ideas. The consensus of modern scholarship is that *The Book of Lord Shang* as we now have it is a compilation of Legalist writings, probably put together gradually over a period of perhaps one hundred years and complete by the third century BC. This judgment is based partly on marked stylistic differences evident in different parts of the text, but also on changes in the content. This is not to say that the work contains inconsistent ideas - indeed its consistency is remarkable – but rather that some sections (notably the last) show considerably more by way of sophistication than do the sections composed earlier. It is reasonable to suppose that these later sections embody the fruit of the experience of applying the Legalist doctrines in practice.

Like Machiavelli's *The Prince* (*Il Principe*, 1532) – a work with which it has often been compared – *The Book of Lord Shang* is a handbook on government, not for the people and not for ministers or officials, but for the ruler alone. Its central purpose is to show the ruler how to succeed: to succeed in ensuring that his state is victorious over others and that his power is never threatened by any other element in the state. (I say 'his' because it is unhistorical to expect any form of sexual equality in these matters at this period in Chinese history.) It is assumed throughout – and this is not surprising in a work from the Warring States Period – that the goal of political activity is the conquest of the whole empire, and the book gives a blueprint showing how to organise the state so as to achieve this objective.

As is the case with all political and moral philosophies, Legalism rests on a particular set of assertions concerning human nature. Philosophers of different schools have over time put forward a wide range of views on this subject, from those who regard human beings as naturally good (unless corrupted by the artifices of civil-isation), via those who hold that human nature is an unformed clay waiting to be formed, to those who regard human beings as fundamentally unpleasant creatures who need to kept sternly in check by their rulers. The Legalists, in common with many political theorists on the right, are firmly in the last group, taking a very dark view of humanity. The position taken in *The Book of Lord Shang* is that human beings are naturally idle, greedy, cowardly, treacherous, unwise and inconsistent: 'The guiding principles of the people are base and they are not consistent in what they value.' (7 *Opening and Debarring*) Any ruler who does not have this constantly in mind is doomed. To assume, as did the followers of Confucius for example, that everyone will respond well if treated with benevolence or goodness (*jen* [*ren*]; cf. *The Analects*, 12, 1), is to be stupidly naive. The only way to control these nasty animals is by using enticement and intimidation, reward and punishment.

The means the ruler must use to administer rewards and punishments is the law (*fa*). The central political recommendation of *The Book of Lord Shang* is that the ruler must establish and maintain a clear, comprehensive and publicly recorded body of law: 'Law is the authoritative principle for the people and is the basis of government; it is what shapes the people. Trying to govern while eliminating the law is like a desire not to be hungry while eliminating food. It is clear enough that there is no hope of realising it.' (*26 The Fixing of Rights and Duties*) The law is to be applied absolutely impartially; ' . . . from ministers of state and generals down to great officers and ordinary folk, whosoever does not obey the king's commands, violates the interdicts of the state, or rebels against the statutes fixed by the ruler, should be guilty of death and should not be pardoned.' (*17 Rewards and Punishments*) This was at the time a revolutionary idea, in direct contradiction to the feudalist way of doing things, where rank and kinship, for example, would be held to be legitimate factors to weigh when considering punishment. Equally revolutionary was the idea that the ruler should create a special class of officials – the first law officers proper in Chinese history – whose duty it was to learn the law by heart and to interpret the law in the event of any ambiguity being discovered in it. (*26 The Fixing of Rights and Duties*)

The punishments embodied in the legal system must be severe. It is taken for granted in Legalist writings that such an approach is a successful means of deterring potential law-breakers. The ultimate goal of such a system, which may seem paradoxical at first sight, is to create a situation in which the laws are never infringed and so, in a sense, there is no need for punishments: 'In applying punishments, light offences should be punished heavily; if light offences do not appear, heavy offences will not come. This is said to be abolishing penalties by means of penalties, and if penalties are abolished, affairs will succeed.' (*13 Making Orders Strict*) Once established, such a system of punishments maintains itself, and as we shall have reason to note again presently, the stability promised by such an arrangement was a prime desideratum in all the sets of political nostrums formulated in this period of Chinese history.

Further, if the system maintains itself, the ruler − like the ideal commander in *The Art of War* and the Taoist sage on which he is modelled − can withdraw from the detail of administration, and be aloof, mysterious and seemingly inactive. (For more information on the Taoist sage, see Lao Tzu's *Tao te ching* in the Suggestions for Further Reading, below.)

This system of impartial laws imposing rigorous punishments for even slight misdemeanours is held to have a number of other beneficial features. For one thing, it creates an atmosphere which is not conducive to two of the most destructive aspects of court life, flattery and slander: ' . . . if people control each other by law and recommend each other by following systematic rules, then they cannot benefit each other with praise nor harm each other with slander.' (*25 Attention to Law*) Again, the system has stability built in as a structural feature. A further consequence of this is that, if the law is clear and rigorously administered, then the system does not need persons of special intelligence, wisdom or insight to run it. It will almost run itself: 'The way to administer a country well, is for the law for the officials to be clear; therefore one does not rely on intelligent and thoughtful men.' (*3 Agriculture and War*) What Legalist theory offers, then, is a strong political system with the stability needed to make the state secure built into it. In other words, it embodies the dream of those suffering under the conditions of life in the Warring States Period.

It will be recalled that another feature of the earlier feudal system of Chinese society was the existence of a number of centres of power and influence in the state, principally in the form of the noble families and their *li* or customs. To the Legalists, this state of affairs was a recipe for political failure. It is assumed throughout *The Book of Lord Shang* that there must be absolute centralisation of power in the hands of the ruler, and that no standards other than those embodied in the law are to be tolerated within the state. This assumption lies behind several further important recommendations in this text. For example, it entails the view which is the subject of *20 Weakening the People*, i.e. ensuring that they have no political power: 'A weak people means a strong state and a strong state means a weak people.' If the people have no power and are dependent on the ruler for any reward, they will be obedient to the law and so of ready service to the state.

Again, if the only standards of conduct which are to be tolerated are those embodied in the law, it follows that any alternatives, in the form of ancient customs or the moral beliefs put forward by philosophers of other schools – which at this period meant especially the followers of Confucius – are to be expunged from the state: no rivals to the law are to be tolerated. Thus in direct contrast to a number of other schools of thought current at the time, the Legalists will have no truck with the beliefs that there was once a golden age in the past when men were wise and good, or that the route to success is to follow their example. *The Book of Lord Shang* attacks this outlook in its opening paragraph: 'Former generations did not follow the same doctrines, so what antiquity should one imitate? The emperors and kings did not copy one another, so what rites should we follow . . . There is more than one way to govern the world and there is no necessity to imitate antiquity, in order to take appropriate measures for the state.' (*1 The Reform of the Law*)

The same belief that the law must be the unique source of values in the state entails the Legalist attack on rival philosophies in general and Confucianism in particular. It would be possible, for example, for someone following Confucian principles to put private duty before obligations to the state, a situation which diminishes the authority of the law and which, if practised on any scale, would weaken the state. Hence the repeated attacks in Legalist texts on the whole system of Confucian values and the cultural apparatus on which it rested, e.g. the study of the ancient texts such as *The Book of Odes* (*Shih Ching* [*Shijing*]) and the *Book of History* (*Shu Ching* [*Shujing*]), works often cited as authoritative by Confucians in any argument. The elements of the Confucianist ethical and cultural programme are regularly referred to by Legalists as vermin, or as in the present text, as parasites. The parasites are: 'rites and music, odes and history, moral culture and virtue, filial piety and brotherly love, sincerity and faith, chastity and integrity, benevolence and righteousness, criticism of the army and being ashamed of fighting. If there are these twelve things . . . the state will be so poor that it will be dismembered.' (*13 Making Orders Strict.* cf *Han Fei Tzu* section 49) It follows further that those who try to make a living from being cultivated, well read in the ancient classics and schooled in Confucianism, i.e. the class of the literati, are not to be tolerated in the state. They are at best passengers and at worst generators of sedition. (For more information on Confucius and Confucianism, see Suggestions for Further Reading.)

All the citizens in the state must be made to engage in its service. They must all have their births registered, so that none can dodge the column (*4 The Elimination of Strength*), and must all in some way be made to contribute to the two activities on which the survival of the state depends, namely agriculture and war. If either of these two activities is neglected, the state will be dismembered. Many of the social and economic policies advocated in the present text rest on this belief. Thus it is recommended that success in agriculture and arms are to be the only routes to reward. Conversely, attempts to avoid duties in either area are to be a certain road to the death penalty (*3 Agriculture and War*). Again, there are to be heavy tax burdens on any citizen who tries to make a profit while not being a producer of food or a soldier – all merchants, entrepreneurs and middlemen of all kinds are parasites and to be held in contempt. Measures must be taken to see that all the cultivable land is brought into use, and that the food thus produced is stored within the borders of the state. Exports are to be discouraged by punitive tariffs while imports are encouraged. Similarly, emigration is discouraged, and immigration, which swells the number of useful citizens in the state (*15 The Encouragement of Immigration*), is encouraged.

With regard to the army, military discipline must be of the utmost strictness: as in the army of Frederick the Great of Prussia, for example, the troops must fear the discipline of their own side more than death at the hands of the enemy. *The Book of Lord Shang* recommends that soldiers be organised into squads of five. If any one of the five is killed in battle, the rest are to be beheaded. Conversely, if a soldier brings back the head of an enemy, he is to be rewarded by exemption from taxes. And there are further detailed rules for rewards and punishments for soldiers (*19 Within the Borders*). In times of war, the whole population can be conscripted and organised into separate armies with distinct roles (*12 Military Defence*).

Brutal though this entire system is in many ways, it has one feature which is far more congenial to modern minds. It is strictly meritocratic. Appointment to high office, and indeed any other form of reward, is to be granted only on the ground of proven ability in the service of the state. There is no room here for hereditary entitlement to office or an old boy network: 'In neither high nor low offices should there be an automatic hereditary succession to the office, rank, lands or emoluments of officials.' (*17 Rewards and Punishments*) What the state needs are the ablest people in the right positions. Inefficiency is the road to political failure, and there is no room in this system for duffers, however well-born. It will be obvious by now that this was again a revolutionary proposal at the time, almost the exact converse of the feudal system.

Equally forward-looking (though entirely consonant with the Legalists' attitude to history noted above) is the last important recommendation we need take note of in *The Book of Lord Shang*. This is the need to review political circumstances constantly. Situations rarely stay stable for long, and any ruler who does not adapt himself to the prevailing conditions is likely soon to find himself deposed and his state dismembered by ambitious neighbours. Any state which falls under the dead hand of practices and institutions so hallowed or set in stone that they cannot be changed if need be will fail. Consistently with this view, the Legalists insist that even the law, the cornerstone of the state, must be changed if necessary: 'When laws are fixed without looking to the customs of the times and without examining the fundamental things of the state, then the people will be in disorder, affairs will be troublesome, so that results will be few.' (*6 The Calculation of Land*)

Such in outline are the major doctrines of Legalism as they are set out in *The Book of Lord Shang*. The basic ideas were added to and given different emphases by later thinkers in the same school, and received their final complex synthesis in the work of Han Fei. In the *Han Fei Tzu*, the doctrines concerning law from the present text are adopted more or less unchanged, but they are supplemented by other views held to be no less important for good government. These additional views centre chiefly on two other concepts, *shih* [*shi*], variously rendered as power, authority or political purchase, and *shu* or statecraft, the ways of handling people a ruler must master in order to succeed. Han Fei's general position, then, is that there is rather more to being a successful ruler than simply the use of law, though the use of law is undoubtedly necessary.

As to the practical efficacy of the views put forward in *The Book of Lord Shang* there can be no doubt. The state of Ch'in adopted them, with the result that Ch'in overwhelmed its neighbours and united China under one ruler, the first Ch'in Emperor, Ch'in Shih-huang-ti [Qin Shihuangdi]. Nor was it only that this dynasty adopted the policies of centralisation, maintaining a strong army, land reform and the creation of an efficient bureaucracy. They adopted in full the anti-cultural programme of the Legalists. As is said in our present text: 'In the state of the intelligent ruler, there is no literature of books and records, but the laws serve as teachings. There are no sayings of early kings, but the officials act as teachers.' (*5 Discussion about the People*) When, notoriously, Ch'in Shih-huang-ti ordered a Burning of the Books in 213 BC, destroying who knows how many works of Chinese culture, he was merely carrying through the Legalist programme. In more ways than one, therefore, the impact of Legalist doctrines on the course of Chinese history has been incalculable.

Their place in the forefront of that history, however, was fairly short-lived. The Ch'in dynasty fell quickly, to be replaced in 206 BC by the Han. For political reasons it suited the Han rulers to distance themselves from full-blown Legalism and they took steps to rehabilitate Confucianism as the 'official' philosophy of the state, a position it was to retain until the fall of the empire. It will be clear, however, that the interest of Legalism is more than merely historical, significant though its historical interest is. The School of Law is an example of an approach to government which tends to repeat itself when circumstances demand it. Whenever a state is threatened with dissolution, or the period is one of intolerable disorder, or both, it often happens that if there is a strong ruler at the time, a set of ruthless, centralising measures not dissimilar to Legalism tends to be suggested, making service to the state mandatory and the central purpose of all citizens. No one aware of modern European history can be ignorant of the possible consequences.

ROBERT WILKINSON

SUGGESTIONS FOR FURTHER READING

Chinese works

Confucius, *The Analects*, Wordsworth, Ware 1996
Han Fei Tzu, *Basic Writings of Han Fei Tzu*, tr. Burton Watson, Columbia University Press, New York 1963
Han Fei Tzu, *The Complete Works of Han Fei Tzu*, tr. W. K. Liao, 2 vols, Probsthain, London 1939 and 1959
Lao Tzu, *Tao te ching*, Wordsworth, Ware 1997
Ssu-ma Ch'ien, *Records of the Grand Historian of China*, tr. Burton Watson, 2 vols, Columbia University Press, New York 1961

Secondary sources

R. T. Ames, *The Art of Rulership: A Study of Ancient Chinese Political Thought*, SUNY Press, Albany 1994
Though primarily a study of a later work of Chinese philosophy, the *Huai Nan Tzu*, this lucid and approachable work contains useful analyses of the central concepts of Legalism, Taoism and Confucianism.
Fung Yu-lan, *A History of Chinese Philosophy* Vol I, tr. D. Bodde, 2nd ed. Princeton University Press 1952
Hsiao Kung-chuan, *A History of Chinese Political Thought*, tr. F. W. Mote, Princeton University Press 1979
Wu Kuo-cheng, *Ancient Chinese Political Theories*, Commercial Press, Shanghai 1933

Also referred to

Niccolò Machiavelli, *The Prince*, Wordsworth, Ware 1997

CHAPTER 1

1 The Reform of the Law

Duke Hsiao discussed his policy. The three great officers, Kung-sun Yang, Kan Lung and Tu Chih, were in attendance on the prince. Their thoughts dwelt on the vicissitudes of the world's affairs; they discussed the principles of rectifying the law, and they sought for the way of directing the people. The prince said: 'Not to forget, at his succession, the tutelary spirits of the soil and of grain, is the way of a prince; to shape the laws and to see to it that an intelligent ruler reigns, are the tasks of a minister. I intend, now, to alter the laws, so as to obtain orderly government, and to reform the rites, so as to teach the people; but I am afraid the empire will criticise me.'

Kung-sun Yang said: 'I have heard it said that he who hesitates in action, does not accomplish anything, and that he who hesitates in affairs, gains no merit. Let Your Highness settle Your thoughts quickly about altering the laws and perhaps not heed the criticism of the empire. Moreover, he who conducts himself as an out-standing man is, as a matter of course, disapproved of by the world; he who has thoughts of independent knowledge is certainly despised by the world. The saying runs: "The stupid do not even understand an affair when it has been completed, but the wise see it even before it has sprouted." One cannot let the people share in the thoughts about the beginnings of an affair, but they should be allowed to share in the rejoicings over the completion of it. The law of Kuo Yen says: "He who is concerned about the highest virtue is not in harmony with popular ideas; he who accomplishes a great work, does not take counsel with the multitude." The law is an expression of love for the people; rites are a means for making things run smoothly. Therefore a sage, if he is able to strengthen the state thereby, does not model himself on antiquity, and if he is able to benefit the people thereby, does not adhere to the established rites.'

Duke Hsiao expressed his approval, but Kan Lung said: 'Not so. I have heard it said: "A sage teaches without changing the people, and a wise man obtains good government without altering the laws." If one teaches in accordance with the spirit of the people, success will be achieved without effort; if one governs, holding on to the law, officials will be well versed in it and the people will live quietly. Now, if Your Highness alters the laws without adhering to the old customs of the Ch'in state, and reforms the rites in order to teach the people, I am afraid that the empire will criticise Your Highness, and I wish that You would reflect maturely.'

Kung-sun Yang replied: 'What you, sir, hold is the point of view of the man-in-the-street. Indeed, ordinary people abide by old practices, and students are immersed in the study of what is reported from antiquity. These two kinds of men are all right for filling offices and for maintaining the law, but they are not the kind who can take part in a discussion which goes beyond the law. The Three Dynasties have attained supremacy by different rites, and the five Lords Protector have attained their protectorships by different laws. Therefore, a wise man creates laws, but a foolish man is controlled by them; a man of talent reforms rites, but a worthless man is enslaved by them. With a man who is enslaved by rites, it is not worth while to speak about matters; with a man who is controlled by laws, it is not worth while to discuss reform. Let Your Highness not hesitate.'

Tu Chih said: 'Unless the advantage be a hundredfold, one should not reform the law; unless the benefit be tenfold, one should not alter an instrument. I have heard it said that in taking antiquity as an example, one makes no mistakes, and in following established rites one commits no offence. Let Your Highness aim at that.'

Kung-sun Yang said: 'Former generations did not follow the same doctrines, so what antiquity should one imitate? The emperors and kings did not copy one another, so what rites should one follow? Fu Hsi and Shen-nung taught but did not punish; Huang-ti, Yao and Shun punished but were not angry; Wen-wang and Wu-wang both established laws in accordance with what was opportune and regulated rites according to practical requirements; as rites and laws were fixed in accordance with what was opportune, regulations and orders were all expedient, and weapons, armour, implements and equipment were all practical. Therefore, I say: "There is more than one way to govern the world and there is no necessity to imitate antiquity, in order to take appropriate measures for the state." T'ang and Wu succeeded in attaining supremacy without following antiquity, and as for the downfall of Yin and Hsia – they were ruined without rites having been altered. Consequently, those who acted counter to antiquity do not necessarily deserve blame, nor do those who followed established rites merit much praise. Let Your Highness not hesitate.'

Duke Hsiao said: 'Excellent! I have heard it said that in poor country districts, much is thought strange, and that in village schools there are many debates. What the foolish laugh about, the wise are sad about; the joy of a madman is the sorrow of a man of talent. One should, in one's plans, be directed by the needs of the times – I have no doubts about it.'

Thereupon, in consequence, he issued the order to bring waste lands under cultivation.

2 An Order to Cultivate Waste Lands

If there is no procrastination in the creating of order, depraved officials have no opportunity of gaining private profits at the expense of the people, nor will the hundred officials be in a condition to temporise and to shift responsibilities on to one another. If the hundred officials are not in a condition to temporise and shift responsibilities on to one another, then agriculture will know days of surplus; and if the depraved officials have no opportunity of gaining private profits at the expense of the people, then agriculture will not be ruined. If agriculture is not ruined, but knows days of surplus, then it is certain waste lands will be brought under cultivation.

If taxes are levied according to the measure of grain, then the ruler will have system and consequently the people will have peace. If the ruler has system, he will be a man of his word, and being a man of his word, the officials will not dare to commit any depravity. If the people have peace, they are circumspect, and being circumspect, they are difficult to move. If the ruler is a man of his word and in consequence the officials dare not commit any depravity, and if the people are circumspect and consequently difficult to move, then there will be no criticism by inferiors of superiors, nor will the officials be regarded as obnoxious. If so, then the able-bodied will be strenuous in agriculture, without changing. If the able-bodied are so, then the youthful will learn it without resting, and when the youthful learn it without resting, it is certain waste lands will be brought under cultivation.

If dignities are not conferred nor office given according to deviating standards, then the people will not prize learning nor, besides, will they hold agriculture cheap. If they do not prize learning, they will be stupid, and being stupid, they will have no interest in outside things; when they have no interest in outside things, the country will exert itself in agriculture and not neglect it, and when the people do not hold agriculture cheap, the country will be peaceful and free from peril. If the country is peaceful and free from peril, exerts itself in agriculture and does not neglect it, then it is certain waste lands will be brought under cultivation.

If salaries are liberal and consequently taxes numerous, then the large number of persons who live on others would mean ruin for agriculture; but if they are assessed according to the calculated number of persons who live on others and are made to work hard, then the wicked and licentious, idle and lazy will have nothing on which to live, and having nothing on which to live, they will take up agriculture; when they take up agriculture, then it is certain waste lands will be brought under cultivation.

Do not allow merchants to buy grain nor farmers to sell grain. If farmers may not sell their grain, then the lazy and inactive ones will exert themselves and be energetic; and, if merchants may not buy grain, then they have no particular joy over abundant years. Having no particular joy over abundant years, they do not make copious profit in years of famine, and making no copious profit, merchants are fearful, and being fearful, they desire to turn farmers. If lazy and inactive farmers exert themselves and become energetic, and if merchants desire to turn farmers, then it is certain waste lands will be brought under cultivation.

If music and fine clothing do not penetrate to all the districts, the people, when they are at work, will pay no attention to the latter, and when they are at rest, will not listen to the former. If, at rest, they do not listen to the one, their spirits will not become licentious; and if, at work, they pay no attention to the other, their minds are concentrated. If their minds are concentrated and their spirits not licentious, then it is certain waste lands will be brought under cultivation.

If it is impossible to hire servants, great prefects and heads of families are not supported and beloved sons cannot eat in laziness. If lazy people cannot be inactive, and hirelings do not find a livelihood, there will certainly be agriculture: when great prefects and heads of families are not supported, agricultural affairs will not suffer; and when beloved sons cannot eat in laziness and lazy people cannot be inactive, then the fields will not lie fallow. If agricultural affairs do not suffer and farmers increase their farming, then it is certain waste lands will be brought under cultivation.

If hostelries for the reception of travellers are abolished, criminals, agitators, conspirators and those who unsettle the minds of the farmers will not travel and in consequence, hotel-keepers will have no means of subsistence. This being so, they will certainly become farmers, and so it is certain waste lands will be brought under cultivation.

If mountains and moors are brought into one hand, then the people who hate agriculture, the tardy and lazy and those who desire double profit, will have no means of subsistence. This being so, they will certainly become farmers, and so it is certain waste lands will be brought under cultivation.

If the prices of wine and meat are made high, and the taxes on them so heavy that they amount to ten times the cost of production, then merchants and retailers will be few, farmers will not be able to enjoy drinking-bouts, and officials will not overeat. If merchants and retailers are few, the ruler does not waste his grain; if the people are unable to enjoy drinking bouts, agriculture will not be neglected; if officials do not overeat, the affairs of the state will not be delayed and the prince will not err in his promotions. If the ruler does not waste the grain and if the people do not neglect agriculture, then it is certain waste lands will be brought under cultivation.

If penalties are made heavy and relations are involved in the punishments, petty and irascible people will not quarrel, intractable and stubborn people will not litigate, slothful and lazy people will not idle, those who waste their substance will not thrive, and those of evil heart, given to flattery, will bring about no change. If these five kinds of people do not appear within the territory, then it is certain waste lands will be brought under cultivation.

If people are not allowed to change their abode unauthorisedly, then stupid and irregular farmers will have no means of subsistence and will certainly turn to agriculture. If the minds of stupid people, full of turbulent desires, have been concentrated, then it is certain farmers will be quiet; if the farmers are quiet and stupid people [turn to agriculture], then it is certain waste lands will be brought under cultivation.

If orders are issued for the service of all younger sons, without exception, the service to last their lifetime, and no high palaces to be built for them, and if orders are given to the grain-measuring officials to weigh out their grain allowance evenly; and if on the one hand they are not used for menial services, but on the other hand they do not necessarily obtain high office, then the younger sons will not be idlers, and (this being so) they will certainly turn to agriculture; and if that is the case, then it is certain waste lands will be brought under cultivation.

If the ministers of state and the great officers are not allowed to occupy themselves with extensive learning, brilliant discussions and idle living, and if they are not allowed to reside, or to travel about, in the various districts, then the farmers will have no opportunity to hear of changes or see different places. This being so, clever farmers will have no opportunity to discard old ways, and stupid farmers will not become clever, nor will they become fond of study. If stupid farmers do not become clever nor fond of study, they will apply themselves energetically to agriculture; and if clever farmers do not discard old ways, then it is certain waste lands will be brought under cultivation.

Women should not be permitted on the market-place of the army, but orders to be there should be given to merchants. Men should be commanded to provide themselves with cuirass and arms, to make the army appear in fine condition. Also if heed is given that there can be no private transport of grain on the army market-place, then there will be no opportunity to hatch corrupt schemes. If those who transport grain dishonestly cannot, from selfish motives, be negligent, frivolous and lazy people will not loiter about the army market-place; and if those who steal grain have no opportunity of selling, and those who send grain can make no private profit, and if frivolous and lazy people do not loiter about the army market-place, then farmers will not be licentious; [if they are not licentious] the government's grain need not be resorted to, and (this being the case) it is certain waste lands will be brought under cultivation.

If the administration of all the districts is of one pattern then [people] will be obedient; eccentric ones will not be able to be ostentatious, and successive officials will not dare to make changes; and if they act wrongly and abolish [the existing administration], it will be impossible to keep their actions hidden. If their mistaken actions do not remain hidden, then among the officials there will be no depraved men; and if eccentric people can not be ostentatious, and successive officials make no changes, then the official appurtenances will be few and the people will not be harassed. If the officials are not depraved, the people will not seek amusement, and if the people do not seek amusement, their occupations will not suffer; if official appurtenances are few, taxes will not be troublesome, and if the people are not harassed, farming will know days of plenty; if farming knows days of plenty, taxes are not troublesome and occupations do not suffer, then it is certain waste lands will be brought under cultivation.

If the tolls at the barriers and on the market are made heavy, then the farmers will hate the merchants, and the merchants will be full of doubt and be unenterprising. If the farmers hate the merchants and the merchants are full of doubt and unenterprising, then it is certain waste lands will be brought under cultivation.

If merchants are made to serve according to their full complement, and if their multitudes of servants and crowds of followers are obliged to be registered, then farmers will have leisure and merchants will be harassed; farmers having leisure, fertile land will not lie fallow; merchants being harassed, the custom of sending presents backwards and forwards will not pervade the various districts. [If fertile land does not lie fallow] farmers will not suffer from famines, [and if the custom of sending presents backwards and forwards does not pervade the various districts], there will be no ostentatious conduct. If farmers do not suffer from famines and there is no ostentatious conduct, then public activities will be pursued with energy, and in the sphere of private activities there will be no fallow fields. [This being so], then agricultural affairs will certainly excel, and this being the case, it is certain waste lands will be brought under cultivation.

If in transporting grain for official use, carters are prohibited from plying for hire and returning with private cargo, and if measures are taken to ensure the registration of carts, oxen, carriages and baggage waggons, the expedition backward and forward will thus be quick and then this occupation will not harm agriculture; agriculture not being harmed, it is certain waste lands will be brought under cultivation.

If it is not permitted to petition officials on behalf of wrongdoers, nor to provide them with food, then criminal people will have no patrons; having no patrons, crimes will not be encouraged; crimes not being encouraged, criminal people will have no hold; criminal people having no hold, farmers will not suffer, and if farmers do not suffer, it is certain waste lands will be brought under cultivation.

3 Agriculture and War

The means whereby a ruler of men encourages the people are office and rank; the means whereby a country is made prosperous are agriculture and war. Now those who seek office and rank, never do so by means of agriculture and war, but by artful words and empty doctrines. That is called 'wearying the people'. The country of those who weary their people will certainly have no strength, and the country of those who have no strength will certainly be dismembered. Those who are capable in organising a country teach the people that office and rank can only be acquired through one opening, and thus, there being no rank without office, the state will do away with fine speaking, with the result that the people will be simple; being simple, they will not be licentious. The people, seeing that the highest benefit comes only through one opening, will strive for concentration, and having concentration, will not be negligent in their occupations. When the people are not negligent in their occupations, they will have much strength, and when they have much strength the state will be powerful.

But now the people within the territory all say that by avoiding agriculture and war, office and rank may be acquired, with the result that eminent men all change their occupations, to apply themselves to the study of the Odes and History and to follow improper standards; on the one hand, they obtain prominence, and on the other, they acquire office and rank. Insignificant individuals will occupy themselves with trade and will practise arts and crafts, all in order to avoid agriculture and war, thus preparing a dangerous condition for the state. Where the people are given to such teachings, it is certain that such a country will be dismembered.

The way to organise a country well is, even though the granaries are filled, not to be negligent in agriculture, and even though the country is large and its population numerous, to have no licence of speech. [This being so], the people will be simple and have concentration; the people being simple and having concentration, then office and rank cannot be obtained by artfulness. If these cannot be obtained by artfulness, then wickedness will not originate; and if wickedness does not originate, the ruler will not be suspicious.

But now the people within the territory, and those who hold office and rank, see that it is possible to obtain, from the court, office and rank by means of artful speech and sophistry. Therefore, there is no permanency in office and rank, with the result that at court they deceive their ruler and, retiring from court, they think of nothing but of how to realise their selfish interests and thus sell power to their inferiors. Now deceiving the ruler and being concerned for their own interests is not to the advantage of the state, but those who thus act, do so for the sake of rank and emolument; selling power to inferiors is not proper for a loyal minister, but those who thus act do so for the sake of insignificant presents.

Consequently all the lower officials, who hope for promotion, say: 'If we send many presents, we may obtain the higher office which we desire.' They say too: 'To strive for promotion, without serving superiors with presents, is like setting a cat as bait for a rat – it is absolutely hopeless. To strive for promotion by serving superiors with sincerity is like wishing to climb a crooked tree by holding on to a broken rope – it is even more hopeless. If, to attain promotion, these two methods are out of the question, what else can we do, in striving for it, but bring the masses below us into action and obtain presents, for the purpose of serving our superiors?'

The people say: 'We till diligently, first to fill the public granaries, and then to keep the rest for the nourishment of our parents; for the sake of our superiors we forget our love of life, and fight for the honour of the ruler and for the peace of the country. But if the granaries are empty, the ruler debased and the family poor, then it is best to seek office. Let us then combine relatives and friends and think of other plans.' Eminent men will apply themselves to the study of the Odes and History, and pursue these improper standards; insignificant individuals will occupy themselves with trade, and practise arts and crafts, all in order to avoid agriculture and war. Where the people are given to such teachings, how can the grain be anything but scarce, and the soldiers anything but weak?

The way to administer a country well, is for the law for the officials to be clear; therefore one does not rely on intelligent and thoughtful men. The ruler makes the people single-minded, and therefore they will not scheme for selfish profit. Then the strength of the country will be consolidated. A country where the strength has been consolidated, is powerful, but a country that loves talking is dismembered. Therefore is it said: 'If there are a thousand people engaged in agriculture and war, and only one in the Odes and History, and clever sophistry, then those thousand will all be remiss in agriculture and war; if there are a hundred people engaged in agriculture and war and only one in the arts and crafts, then those hundred will all be remiss in agriculture and war.

The country depends on agriculture and war for its peace, and likewise the ruler, for his honour. Indeed, if the people are not engaged in agriculture and war, it means that the ruler loves words and that the officials have lost consistency of conduct. If there is consistency of conduct in officials, the country is well-governed; and if single-mindedness is striven after, the country is rich; to have the country both rich and well governed is the way to attain supremacy. Therefore is it said: 'The way to supremacy is no other than by creating single-mindedness!'

However, nowadays the ruler, in his appointments, takes into consideration talent and ability and cleverness and intelligence, and thus clever and intelligent men watch for the likes and dislikes of the ruler, so that officials are caused to transact their business in a way which is adapted to the ruler's mind. As a result there is no consistency of conduct in the officials, the state is in disorder and there is no concentration. Sophists [are honoured] and there is no law. Under such circumstances, how can the people's affairs be otherwise than many, and how can the land be otherwise than fallow?

If, in a country, there are the following ten things: odes and history, rites and music, virtue and the cultivation thereof, benevolence and integrity, sophistry and intelligence, then the ruler has no one whom he can employ for defence and warfare. If a country is governed by means of these ten things, it will be dismembered as soon as an enemy approaches, and even if no enemy approaches, it will be poor. But if a country banishes these ten things, enemies will not dare to approach, and even if they should, they would be driven back. When it mobilises its army and attacks, it will gain victories; when it holds the army in reserve and does not attack, it will be rich. A country that loves strength makes assaults with what is difficult, and thus it will be successful. A country that loves sophistry makes assaults with what is easy, and thus it will be in danger.

Therefore sages and intelligent princes are what they are, not because they are able to go to the bottom of all things, but because they understand what is essential in all things. Therefore the secret of their administration of the country lies in nothing else than in their examination of what is essential. But now, those who run a state for the most part overlook what is essential, and the discussions at court, on government, are confused, and efforts are made to displace each other in them; thus the prince is dazed by talk, officials confused by words, and the people become lazy and will not farm. The result is that all the people within the territory change and become fond of sophistry, take pleasure in study, pursue trade, practise arts and crafts, and shun agriculture and war; and so in this manner [the ruin of the country] will not be far off. When the country has trouble, then because studious people hate law, and merchants are clever in bartering and artisans are useless, the state will be easily destroyed.

Indeed, if farmers are few, and those who live idly on others are many, then the state will be poor and in a dangerous condition. Now, for example, if various kinds of caterpillars, which are born in spring and die in autumn, appear only once, the result is that the people have no food for many years. Now, if one man tills and a hundred live on him, it means that they are like a great visitation of caterpillars. Though there may be a bundle of the Odes and History in every hamlet and a copy in every family, yet it is useless for good government, and it is not a method whereby this condition of things may be reversed. Therefore the ancient kings made people turn back to agriculture and war. For this reason is it said: 'Where a hundred men farm and one is idle, the state will attain supremacy; where ten men farm and one is idle, the state will be strong; where half farms and half is idle, the state will be in peril.' That is why those who govern the country well, wish the people to take to agriculture. If the country does not take to agriculture, then in its quarrels over authority with the various feudal lords, it will not be able to maintain itself, because the strength of the multitude will not be sufficient. Therefore the feudal lords vex its weakness and make use of its state of decadence; and if the territory is invaded and dismembered, without the country being stirred to action, it will be past saving.

A sage knows what is essential in administrating a country, and so he induces the people to devote their attention to agriculture. If their attention is devoted to agriculture, then they will be simple, and being simple, they may be made correct. Being perplexed, it will be easy to direct them; being trustworthy, they may be used for defence and warfare. Being single-minded, opportunities of deceit will be few, and they will attach importance to their homes. Being single-minded, their careers may be made dependent on rewards and penalties; being single-minded, they may be used abroad.

Indeed, the people will love their ruler and obey his commandments even to death, if they are engaged in farming, morning and evening; but they will be of no use if they see that glib-tongued, itinerant scholars succeed in being honoured in serving the prince, that merchants succeed in enriching their families, and that artisans have plenty to live upon. If the people see both the comfort and advantage of these three walks of life, then they will indubitably shun agriculture; shunning agriculture, they will care little for their homes; caring little for their homes, they will certainly not fight and defend these for the ruler's sake.

Generally speaking, in administrating a country, the trouble is when the people are scattered and when it is impossible to consolidate them. That is why a sage tries to bring about uniformity and consolidation. A state where uniformity of purpose has been established for one year, will be strong for ten years; where uniformity of purpose has been established for ten years, it will be strong for a hundred years, where uniformity of purpose has been established for a hundred years, it will be strong for a thousand years; and a state which has been strong for a thousand years will attain supremacy.

An ordinary prince cultivates the system of rewards and penalties in order to support his teaching of uniformity of purpose, and in this way his teaching has permanency and his administration is successfully established. But he who attains supremacy, succeeds in regulating those things which are most essential for the people, and therefore, even without the need of rewards and gifts, the people will love their ruler; without the need of ranks and emoluments, the people will follow their avocations; without the need of penalties, the people will do their duty to the death.

When a country is in peril and the ruler in anxiety, it is of no avail to the settling of this danger for professional talkers to form battalions. The reason why a country is in danger and its ruler in anxiety lies in some strong enemy or in another big state. Now if a prince is unable to vanquish that strong enemy or to destroy that big state, he improves his defences, makes the best use of the topographical conditions, consolidates the strength of the people and thus meets the foreign attack. After this the danger may be averted and supremacy yet attained. That is why an intelligent prince, in improving the administration, strives for uniformity, removes those who are of no use, restrains volatile scholars and those of frivolous pursuits, and makes them all uniformly into farmers. Thereafter the reigning dynasty may become rich and the people's strength may be consolidated.

Nowadays, the rulers of the world are all anxious over the perilous condition of their countries and the weakness of their armies, and they listen at all costs to the professional talkers: but though these may form battalions, talk profusely and employ beautiful expressions, it is of no practical use. When a ruler loves their sophistry and does not seek for their practical value, then the professional talkers have it all their own way, expound their crooked sophistries in the streets, their various groups become great crowds, and the people, seeing that they succeed in captivating kings, dukes and great men, all imitate them. Now, if men form parties, the arguments and dissensions in the country will be of confusing diversity; the lower classes will be amused and the great men will enjoy it, with the result that amongst such a people farmers will be few and those who, in idleness, live on others will be many. These latter being numerous, farmers will be in a perilous position, and this being so, land will be left lying fallow. If study becomes popular, people will abandon agriculture and occupy themselves with debates, high-sounding words and discussions on false premises; abandoning agriculture, they will live on others in idleness, and seek to surpass one another with words. Thus the people will become estranged from the ruler, and there will be crowds of disloyal subjects. This is a doctrine which leads to the impoverishment of the state and to the weakening of the army. Indeed, if a country employs people for their talking, then the people will not be nurtured in agriculture; so it is only an intelligent prince who understands that by fondness for words one cannot strengthen the army nor open up the land. Only when a sage rules the country will he strive for singleness of purpose and for the consolidation of the people in agriculture, and for that alone.

4 The Elimination of Strength

To remove the strong by means of a strong people brings weakness; to remove the strong by means of a weak people brings strength. If the country practises virtue, criminals are many. If the country is rich, but is administered as if it were poor, then it is said to be doubly rich, and the doubly rich are strong. If the country is poor, but is administered as if it were rich, it is said to be doubly poor, and the doubly poor are weak. If its army accomplishes what the enemy dares not accomplish, [a country] is strong; if affairs are undertaken which the enemy is ashamed to perform, [a country] profits. A ruler values many changes, but the country values few changes. If the country has few products it will be dismembered, but if it has many products it will be strong. A country of a thousand chariots that keeps only one outlet for its products will flourish, but if it keeps ten outlets it will be dismembered.

If in war its army is efficient, a country will be strong; but if fighting is disorderly and the army unwilling, the country will be dismembered.

Farming, trade and office are the three permanent functions in a state, and these three functions give rise to six parasitic functions, which are called: care for old age, living on others, beauty, love, ambition and virtuous conduct. If these six parasites find an attachment, there will be dismemberment. The three functions are attached to three different men, but these six functions may attach themselves to one man.

To abolish law by means of the law means strength; to establish law by means of the law means dismemberment. If officials are permanent, law is abolished; but if officials are often transferred, laws are established. In administering a great country, it becomes small; in administering a small country, it becomes great. If the people are made strong, the army will be doubly diminished; if the people are made weak, the army will be doubly strengthened.

Indeed, to attack the strong with a strong people spells ruin; to attack the strong with a weak people means the attainment of supremacy. If the country is strong and war is not waged, the poison will be carried into the territory; rites and music and the parasitic functions will arise, and dismemberment will be inevitable. But if the country (being strong) thereupon wages war, the poison will be carried to the enemy, and not suffering from rites and music and the parasitic functions, it will be strong. If those who exert themselves are promoted, and men of merit are employed in office, the country will be strong; but if the parasitic functions arise, dismemberment will be inevitable. If farmers are few and merchants numerous, men in high positions will be poor, merchants will be poor and farmers will be poor; these three functions all being poor, dismemberment is inevitable.

If in a country there are the following ten evils: rites, music, odes, history, virtue, moral culture, filial piety, brotherly duty, integrity and sophistry, the ruler cannot make the people fight and dismemberment is inevitable; and this brings extinction in its train. If the country has not these ten things and the ruler can make the people fight, he will be so prosperous that he will attain supremacy. A country where the virtuous govern the wicked, will suffer from disorder, so that it will be dismembered; but a country where the wicked govern the virtuous, will be orderly, so that it will become strong.

A country which is administered by the aid of odes, history, rites, music, filial piety, brotherly duty, virtue and moral culture, will, as soon as the enemy approaches, be dismembered; if he does not approach, the country will be poor. But if a country is administered without these eight,[1] the enemy dares not approach, and even if he should, he would certainly be driven off; when it mobilises its army and attacks, it will capture its objective, and having captured it, will be able to hold it; when it holds its army in reserve, and makes no attack, it will be rich. A country that loves force is said to attack with what is difficult; a country that loves words is said to attack with what is easy. A country that attacks with what is difficult will gain ten points for every one point that it undertakes, whereas a country that attacks with what is easy will lose a hundred men for every ten that it marches out.

1 Here eight things are mentioned instead of ten; perhaps the last two have been forgotten in copying and the character 'ten' later altered into eight.

If penalties are made heavy and rewards light, the ruler loves his people and they will die for him; but if rewards are made heavy and penalties light, the ruler does not love his people, nor will they die for him. When, in a prosperous country, penalties are applied, the people will reap profit and at the same time stand in awe; when rewards are applied, the people will reap profit and at the same time have love.

A country that has no strength and that practises knowledge and cleverness, will certainly perish; but a fearful people, stimulated by penalties, will become brave, and a brave people, encouraged by rewards, will fight to the death. If fearful people become brave and brave people fight to the death, [the country will have no match]; having no match, it will be strong, and being strong it will attain supremacy.

If the poor are encouraged by rewards, they will become rich, and if penalties are applied to the rich, they will become poor. When in administrating a country one succeeds in making the poor rich and the rich poor, then the country will have much strength, and this being the case, it will attain supremacy.

In a country that has supremacy, there are nine penalties as against one reward; in a strong country, there will be seven penalties to three rewards, and in a dismembered country, there will be five penalties to five rewards.

A country where uniformity of purpose has been established for one year, will be strong for ten years; where uniformity of purpose has been established for ten years, it will be strong for a hundred years; where uniformity of purpose has been established for a hundred years, it will be strong for a thousand years; and a country that has been strong for a thousand years will attain supremacy.

One who has prestige captures ten by means of one, and grasps concrete things by means of the very sound of his name. Therefore he who succeeds in having prestige, attains supremacy.

A country which knows how to produce strength but not how to reduce it, may be said to be a country that attacks itself, and it is certain that it will be dismembered; but a country that knows how to produce strength and how to reduce it may be said to be one that attacks the enemy, and it is certain that it will become strong. Therefore, the combating of the parasites, the curtailing of its energies and the attacking of its enemy – if a country employs two of these methods and sets aside only one, it will be strong; but that which employs all three methods will have so much prestige that it will attain supremacy.

A country where ten hamlets are the smallest unit for judgments, will be weak; a country where nine hamlets are the smallest unit for judgments, will be strong. He who can create order in one day will attain supremacy; he who creates order in a night will be strong, and he who procrastinates in creating order will have his state dismembered.

If the whole population is registered at birth and erased at death, there would be no people who would escape agriculture, and in the fields there would be no fallow land. Thus the country would be rich, and being rich it would be strong. If penalties are removed by means of penalties, the country will enjoy order, but if penalties are set up by means of penalties, the country will be in disorder. Therefore is it said: 'In applying penalties, punish heavily the light offences.' If punishments are abolished, affairs will succeed and the country will be strong. But if heavy offences are punished heavily and light offences lightly, penalties will appear, trouble will arise and such a state will be dismembered. Punishment produces force, force produces strength, strength produces awe, awe produces kindness. Kindness has its origin in force.

In exerting force one should fight with complete courage, and in fighting, plan with complete wisdom.

The appearance of gold means the disappearance of grain, and the appearance of grain means the disappearance of gold. If products are cheap – those who occupy themselves with agriculture being many, and buyers being few – farmers will be in hard straits and wickedness will be encouraged, so that the army will be weak and the state will certainly be dismembered and come to extinction.

For every ounce of gold appearing within its borders, twelve *piculs* of grain will disappear abroad; but for every twelve *piculs* of grain appearing within its borders, one ounce of gold will disappear abroad. If a country favours the appearance of gold within its borders, then gold and grain will both disappear, granary and treasury will both be empty, and the state will be weak. But if a country favours the appearance of grain within its borders, then gold and grain will both appear, granary and treasury will both be filled, and the state will be strong.

A strong country knows thirteen figures: the number of granaries within its borders, the number of able-bodied men and of women, the number of old and of weak people, the number of officials and of officers, the number of those making a livelihood by talking, the number of useful people, the number of horses and of oxen, the quantity of fodder and of straw. If he who wishes to make his country strong, does not know these thirteen figures, though his geographical position may be favourable and the population numerous, his state will become weaker and weaker, until it is dismembered.

A country where there are no dissatisfied people is called a strong country. When the army is mobilised for an offensive, rank is given according to military merit, and reliance being placed upon the military, victory is certain. When the army is in reserve and agriculture is pursued, rank is given according to the production of grain, and reliance being placed upon farming, the country will be rich. If in military enterprises the enemy is conquered and if, when the army is in reserve, the country becomes rich, then it attains supremacy.

CHAPTER 2

5 Discussion about the People

Sophistry and cleverness are an aid to lawlessness; rites and music are symptoms of dissipations and licence; kindness and benevolence are the foster-mother of transgressions; employment and promotion are opportunities for the rapacity of the wicked. If lawlessness is aided, it becomes current; if there are symptoms of dissipation and licence, they will become the practice; if there is a foster-mother for transgressions, they will arise; if there are opportunities for the rapacity of the wicked, they will never cease. If these eight things come together, the people will be stronger than the government; but if these eight things are non-existent in a state, the government will be stronger than the people. If the people are stronger than the government, the state is weak; if the government is stronger than the people, the army is strong. For if these eight things exist, the ruler has no one to use for defence and war, with the result that the state will be dismembered and will come to ruin; but if there are not these eight things, the ruler has the wherewithal for defence and war, with the result that the state will flourish and attain supremacy.

If virtuous officials are employed, the people will love their own relatives, but if wicked officials are employed, the people will love the statutes. To agree with, and to respond to, others is what the virtuous do; to differ from, and to spy upon, others is what the wicked do. If the virtuous are placed in positions of evidence, transgressions will remain hidden; but if the wicked are employed, crimes will be punished. In the former case the people will be stronger than the law; in the latter, the law will be stronger than the people. If the people are stronger than the law, there is lawlessness in the state, but if the law is stronger than the people, the army will be strong. Therefore is it said: 'Governing through good people leads to lawlessness and dismemberment; governing through wicked people leads to order and strength.' A country which attacks with what is difficult will gain ten points for every one that it undertakes; a country which attacks with what is easy will lose a hundred men for every ten that it marches out. A country that loves force is said to attack with what is difficult; a country that loves words is said to attack with what is easy. People find it easy to talk, but difficult to serve. A state where, when the laws of the country are applied, conditions for the people are hard and by military service those conditions are eased, so that it attacks with force, will gain ten points for every one it undertakes; but a state where, when the laws of the country are applied, conditions for the people are easy, and by military service those conditions are made hard, so that it attacks with words, will lose a hundred men for every ten that it marches out.

The fact that penalties are heavy makes rank the more honourable, and the fact that rewards are light makes punishments the more awe-inspiring. If rank is honoured, the ruler loves the people, and if punishments are so awe-inspiring, the people still die for their ruler. Therefore, in a prosperous country, the people profit by the application of penalties, and by the distribution of rewards the ruler will gain credit.

If the law goes into details, the punishments will be multitudinous; if the laws are multitudinous, punishments will be scarce.

If, from a condition of rule and order, the people become lawless, and if one tries to rule this lawlessness, it will only increase; therefore, it should be ruled while it is still in a state of rule and order, then there will be true rule and order; if it is ruled while it is in a state of lawlessness, lawlessness will remain.

It is the nature of the people to be orderly, but it is circumstances that cause disorder. Therefore, in the application of punishments, light offences should be regarded as serious; if light offences do not occur, serious ones have no chance of coming. This is said to be 'ruling the people while in a state of law and order'.

If, in the application of punishments, serious offences are regarded as serious, and light offences as light, light offences will not cease and in consequence, there will be no means of stopping the serious ones. This is said to be 'ruling the people while in a state of lawlessness'. So, if light offences are regarded as serious, punishments will be abolished, affairs will succeed and the country will be strong; but if serious offences are regarded as serious and light ones as light, then punishments will appear; moreover, trouble will arise and the country will be dismembered.

If the people are brave, they should be rewarded with what they desire; if they are timorous, they should be put to death in a manner they hate. In this way timorous people, being incited by punishments, will become brave; and the brave, being encouraged by rewards, will fight to the death. If timorous people become brave, and the brave fight to the death, the country having no equal will certainly attain supremacy.

If the people are poor, they are weak; if the country is rich, they are licentious, and consequently there will be the parasites; the parasites will bring weakness. Therefore, the poor should be benefited with rewards, so that they become rich, and the rich should be injured by punishments, so that they become poor. The important thing in undertaking the administration of a country is to make the rich poor, and the poor rich. If that is effected, the country will be strong. If the three classes of people do not suffer from the parasites, the country will be strong for a long time to come, and such a country, free of parasites, may be certain of supremacy.

Punishment produces force, force produces strength, strength produces awe, awe produces virtue. Virtue has its origin in punishments. For the more punishments there are, the more valued are rewards, and the fewer rewards there are, the more heed is paid to punishments, by virtue of the fact that people have desires and dislikes. What they desire are the six kinds of licence,[1] and what they dislike are the four kinds of hardship.[2] Indulgence in these six kinds of licence will make the country weak; but the practice of these four kinds of hardship will make the army strong. Therefore, in a country which has attained supremacy, punishments are applied in nine cases and rewards in one. If punishments are applied in nine cases, the six kinds of licence will stop, and if in one case rewards are given, the four kinds of hardship will be practised. If the six kinds of licence are stopped, the country will be without crime; and if the four kinds of hardship are practised, the army will be without equal.

1 i.e. the six parasitic functions as enumerated in section 4.
2 Probably shame, disgrace, labour and hardship, mentioned in section 6.

The things which the people desire are innumerable, but that from which they benefit is one and the same thing. Unless the people be made one, there is no way to make them attain their desire. Therefore, they are unified; as a result of this unification, their strength is consolidated, and in consequence of this consolidation, they are strong; if, being strong, they are made use of, they are doubly strong. Therefore, a country that knows how to produce strength and how to reduce it is said to be 'one that attacks the enemy', and is sure to become strong. It bars all private roads for gratifying their ambition, and opens only one gate through which they can attain their desire; thus, without doubt, it can make the people first do what they hate, in order thereafter to reach what they desire; and so their strength will be great. If their strength is great, but not made use of, ambition is gratified; and this being so, there will be private interest and in consequence there will be weakness.

Therefore, a country that knows how to produce strength, but not how to reduce it, is said to be 'one that attacks itself', and it is certain to be dismembered. So it is said that if a state has attained supremacy, it does not reserve its strength and the family does not hoard grain. That the state does not reserve its strength means that its subjects are used, and that the family does not hoard grain means that the superiors keep it in the granaries.

If the order of the country depends on the judgments of the family, it attains supremacy; if it depends on the judgments of the officials, it becomes only strong; if it depends on the judgments of the prince, it becomes weak. If light offences are heavily punished, punishments will disappear; if officials are permanent, there is orderly administration. The necessary guarantee for restricting the use of punishments is that promises of rewards are kept. If they make it their habit to denounce all crimes, then the people make the judgments in their own minds; and if, when the ruler gives his orders, the people know how to respond, so that the means for enforcing the law are really manufactured in the families and merely applied by the officials, then the judgments over affairs rest with the family. Therefore, in the case of one who attains supremacy, judgments with regard to punishments and rewards rest with the people's own minds, and those with regard to the application of the means for enforcing the law rest with the family. If there is a clear law, people will agree with one another; if there is an obscure law, people will differ from one another. If they agree, things run smoothly, but if they differ, things are hampered; in the former case, there is order, in the latter, disorder. If there is order, it is the families that make judgements; if there is disorder, it is the prince who makes judgments.

Those who administer a country deem it important that inferiors should give judgments; therefore, when ten hamlets are the unit for making judgments, there will be weakness; whereas when five hamlets are the unit for making judgments, there will be strength. If it is the family that gives judgments, there will be abundance. Therefore, of such a country it is said: 'He who creates order in one day will attain supremacy.' If it is the officials who give judgments, the order will not be sufficient; therefore of such a country it is said: 'He who creates order in a night will merely be strong.' But if it is the prince who gives judgments, there will be disorder; therefore of such a country it is said: 'He who procrastinates in creating order will be dismembered.'

Therefore in a country that has the true way, order does not depend on the prince, and the people do not merely follow the officials.

6 The Calculation of Land

The disasters of the rulers of the world generally come from their not measuring their strength in the use of armies, and from their not measuring their territory in managing the grass-fields and uncultivated lands. Therefore, sometimes the territory is narrow and the population numerous, so that the population exceeds the territory; or sometimes the territory is extensive, but the population sparse, so that the territory exceeds the population. If the population exceeds the territory, then one should pay attention to opening up new land; if the territory exceeds the population, then one should set about calling in colonists. By opening up new land, one effects increase . . . [1] If the population exceeds the territory, then the achievements of the state will be few and the military strength small; if the territory exceeds the population, then the resources of mountains and moors will not be utilised. Now, to neglect natural resources and to pander to the people's dissipations is to fail in one's duty as a ruler, and when high and low act thus, then in spite of a large population, the army will be weak, and in spite of a big territory, its strength will be small.

In administering a state therefore, and in disposing of its territory, the correct rule of the former kings was to populate the mountains and forests with a tenth of the people, the marshes and moors with a tenth, the valleys, dales and streams with a tenth, cities, towns and highways with four tenths.[2] In administering a state, therefore, and in dividing arable land, if a minimum of 500 *mu* is sufficient to support one soldier, it is not making proper use of the land. But if a territory of 100 square *li* supports 10,000 soldiers for war as a minimum, then it shows that the cultivated

1 There seems to be a gap in the text.
2 The text seems to be defective: in section 15. a parallel text runs: 'cities, towns and highways with one tenth, barren fields with one tenth, fertile fields with four tenths.'

land is sufficient to nourish its population, that cities, towns and highways are sufficient to accommodate their inhabitants, that mountains and forests, marshes and moors, valleys and dales, are sufficient to provide profit, and that marshes and moors, dykes and embankments are sufficient for grazing. Therefore, when the army marches out and grain is given them, there is still a surplus of riches; when the army is resting and the people at work, the cattle are always sufficient. This is said to be the rule for making use of the land and for supporting soldiers. But nowadays, although the rulers of the world have territory of several thousand square *li*, the produce is not sufficient to support the soldiers and to fill the granaries, and the army is equalled by the neighbours. I regret this state of affairs, therefore, on behalf of the ruler. Indeed, having a large territory and not cultivating it is like having no territory; having a numerous population, but not employing it, is like having no population.

Therefore, the statistical method of administering a country is to give attention to the cultivation of the grass lands; the way to employ the soldiers is to pay attention to making uniform rewards. If private gain has been debarred in outside occupations, then the people will be concerned with keeping to agriculture. If they keep to agriculture, they will be simple, and if they are simple, they fear the law. If private rewards are forbidden to those below, then the people will take the offensive forcibly against the enemy, and by taking the offensive against him, they conquer. How does one know that it will be thus? Well, the natural disposition of the people is that if they are simple, they will produce hard work and will exert their strength easily. If they are poor, they will develop common sense and give due consideration to what is profitable. If they exert their strength easily, they will think lightly of death and will enjoy employment in warfare. If they give due consideration to what is profitable, they will fear punishment and will easily suffer hardship; if they easily suffer hardship, then the capacity of the soil will be developed to the full; if they enjoy employment in warfare, military strength will be developed to the utmost.

Now, if he who administers a country is able to develop the capacity of the soil to the full and to cause the people to fight to the death, then fame and profit will jointly accrue.

It is the nature of the people, when they are hungry, to strive for food; when they are tired, to strive for rest; when they suffer hardship, to seek enjoyment; when they are in a state of humiliation, to strive for honour. Such is the natural disposition of the people. If the people strive for gain, then they lose the rules of polite behaviour; if they strive for fame, they lose the eternal principles of human nature. How can we conclude that it is so? Well, take now robbers and thieves; they infringe the interdicts of the prince, above, and below they fail in the polite behaviour of subject and son. Therefore, though their reputations are dishonoured and their persons endangered, yet because of the profit they do not desist. Above these are the scholars of the world; their clothes do not warm their skins, their food does not fill their stomachs, they travail their thoughts, fatigue their four limbs and suffer in their five internal organs, and yet they go on increasing their activity. This is not prompted by the eternal principles of human nature, but for the sake of fame. Therefore is it said: 'Where fame and profit meet, that is the way the people will follow.' If the ruler controls the handle of fame and profit, so as to be able to acquire success and fame, it is due to statistical method. A sage examines the weights, in order to control the handle of the scales; he examines the statistical method in order to direct the people. Statistics is the true method of ministers and rulers and the essential of a state. For never yet has it happened but that a state of a thousand chariots that neglected statistics has come into a perilous position, and ministers and rulers that neglected method have experienced disorder.

Nowadays, the rulers of the world wish to open up their territory and to govern the population, without examining the statistics, and ministers desire to fulfil their task without establishing a method. Therefore, the country has a disobedient population and the ruler refractory ministers.

A sage, therefore, in organising a country causes the people in home affairs to adhere to agriculture, and in foreign affairs to scheme for war. Now, agriculture makes the people suffer hardships, and war makes them run dangers, and the means whereby they can be led to encounter hardships and to perform actions that expose them to danger, is calculation. For the people, when alive, scheme for profit, and when in danger of death, are anxious for fame.

It is necessary to examine whence fame and profit spring. If the profit comes from the soil, then people will use their strength to the full; if fame results from war, then they will fight to the death. Now if, at home, the people are directed to use their strength to the full, then the fields will not lie fallow; and if, abroad, they are directed to fight to the death, then they conquer their enemies. If enemies are conquered and at the same time fields do not lie fallow, then without moving, the result will be obtained of having both wealth and strength.

But nowadays, it is not thus; that which the rulers of the world are particularly concerned about is not at all that of which the state stands in urgent need. In their persons, they have the conduct of Yao and Shun, but in their results they do not even approximate those of T'ang or Wu. The mistake lies with the handle which they hold. Let me be permitted to set forth their error.

In administrating the country, they reject power and indulge in talking. By talking, their persons become cultivated, but their success is small. So scholars, full of empty talk about the Odes and the Book of History, are held in esteem, so that people become restless and think lightly of their prince; scholars who are out of office are held in esteem, so that people become estranged and criticise their superiors; braves are held in esteem, so that the people become quarrelsome and think lightly of prohibitions; artisans are used, so that the people become volatile and easily move their places of abode; merchants and retailers, though leisurely, yet make profit, so that the people follow their example and discuss their superiors. Therefore, if these five kinds of people are used in the state, then fields will lie fallow and the army will be weak. The capital of scholars who are full of empty words lies in their mouths; that of scholars who are out of office lies in their ideas; that of braves in their valour, that of artisans in their hands, and that of merchants and retailers in their bodies. Thus, they can carry their personal capital round to any house on earth. If, for the people's capital, importance is attached to physical talents, and for their habitat they are dependent on the outside world, then those who carry considerable capital will become temporary sojourners. This would have caused difficulties even to Yao and Shun; therefore, T'ang and Wu prohibited it, with the result that their success was established and their fame made.

A sage cannot, with what the world thinks easy, overcome that which it thinks difficult, but he must, by means of what it thinks difficult, overcome that which it thinks easy. So, for example, if the people are stupid, he can overcome it by means of knowledge; if the world is educated, he can overcome it by means of force. When people are stupid, they think force easy, but cleverness difficult; but if the world is clever, then it thinks knowledge easy, but force difficult. So, when Shen-nung taught ploughing and attained supreme sway, the leadership was by means of his knowledge. When T'ang and Wu made themselves strong and attacked the feudal lords, the subjugation was by means of force. Nowadays, the world is full of cleverness and people are dissolute, and at this juncture, when the times of T'ang and Wu are imitated, to practise the actions of Shen-nung . . . thus a country of a thousand chariots hereby falling into a state of disorder:[3] This is paying particular attention to the wrong things.

It is people's nature, when measuring, to take the longest part, when weighing, to take the heaviest, when adjusting the scales, to seek profit. If an intelligent prince watches these three things diligently, order may be established in the country and the capacities of the people may be utilised. If the state makes few demands from the people, then the people will make many evasions from those demands. Direct the people at home to adhere to farming, and abroad to be concentrated in warfare. Therefore, a sage's way of administering a country is to prohibit much, in order to limit the people's capacity, and to rely on force in order to render trickeries powerless. These two methods being used in combination, people within the borders will be single-minded; being single-minded, they will farm; farming, they will be simple and being simple, they will dwell quietly and dislike going out. Therefore, a sage's way of ordering a country is that the people's capital should be stored in the soil, and that dangers should be run abroad by borrowing a temporary habitat.

If their capital lies in the soil, they will be simple, and if, by borrowing a temporary habitat abroad, dangers would be run, they will be anxious. If at home the people are simple, and abroad they

3 The text seems corrupt here.

are anxious, then as a result they will exert themselves in farming and be alert in warfare. If the people are zealous in farming, then their capital will be considerable; if they are alert in warfare, the neighbouring states will be in danger. If their capital is considerable, then they can not carry it on their backs[4] and go elsewhere; if the neighbouring states are in danger, they will not go where there is no capital, for to go to a place of danger and to borrow a habitat outside – even a madman does not do such a thing.

Therefore a sage, in ordering a country, looking to popular custom, fixes their laws with the result that there is order, and examining the state, gives his attention to what is fundamental,[5] with the result that everything is fitting. When laws are fixed without looking to the customs of the times and without examining the fundamental things of the state, then the people will be in disorder, affairs will be troublesome, so that results will be few.

This is what I call error.

Now the idea of punishments is to restrain depravity, and the idea of rewards is to support the interdicts. Shame and disgrace, labour and hardship are what the people dislike;[6] fame and glory, ease and joy are what the people pay attention to. So, if the penalties of the country are such that they do not cause dislike, and the titles and emoluments are not worth attention, it is an omen of the ruin of the country. If culprits often escape through the meshes, inferior people will be depraved and dissolute and will not think of the punishments as deterrents, and thus they will be applied to the people in a haphazard manner. That being so, and the way to fame and glory by means of gain not being one, then superior men will apply power to obtain a name and inferior people will not avoid what is prohibited. Therefore, the punishments will be numerous. If the superior man[7] does not set up his commands clearly, minor penalties will be applied. If punishments are numerous and minor penalties are applied, the country will have many criminals.[8] Then

---

4 Like small merchants or pedlars.

5 i.e. agriculture.

6 cf. section 5, where four kinds of hardship are mentioned.

7 Here meaning the prince.

8 The text is not very clear, but the meaning seems to be that there should be system in the punishments.

the rich will not be able to keep their wealth, nor the poor to apply themselves to their occupations; the fields will lie fallow and the state will be poor.

If the fields lie fallow, the people will live by deceit; if the country is poor, the ruler will lack rewards. Therefore, when a sage administers a country, culprits have no government position and felons do not hold office. If culprits were to hold rank, then the superior man would resign from his position; if felons were to be clothed with brocades and fed with meat, then the inferior man would hope for such advantages. If superior men resigned from their positions, one would be ashamed of merit; if inferior men hoped for such advantages, one would boast of wickedness. So punishments and executions are the means whereby wickedness is stopped, and office and rank are the means whereby merit is encouraged.

Nowadays, people spurn the ranks established by the state, and laugh at the punishments set up by it. This evil is caused by the law and method followed. Therefore, the superior man, in handling his authority, unifies the government in order to fix his methods; in establishing offices, he makes rank valuable, to correspond with them, and he makes his appointments, taking people's exertions into account and according to their merit, so that the balance between high and low is even. When this is the case, ministers will be able to exert their strength to the uttermost and the ruler to exercise autocratic sway.

7 Opening and Debarring

During the time when heaven and earth were established, and the people were produced, people knew their mothers but not their fathers. Their way was to love their relatives and to be fond of what was their own. From loving their relatives came discrimination, and from fondness of what was their own, insecurity. As the people increased and were preoccupied with discrimination and insecurity, they fell into disorder. At that time, people were intent on excelling others, and subjected each other by means of force; the former led to quarrels, and the latter to disputes. If in disputes there were no justice, no one would be satisfied; therefore men of talent established equity and justice and instituted unselfishness, so that people began to talk of moral virtue. At that time, the idea of loving one's relatives began to disappear, and that of honouring talent arose.

Now virtuous men are concerned with love, and the way of talented men is to vie with one another. As people increased and were not restrained, and had for long been in the way of vying with one another, there was again disorder. Therefore a sage, who received the administration, made divisions of land and property, of men and women. Divisions having been established, it was necessary to have restraining measures, so he instituted interdicts. These being instituted, it was necessary to have those who could enforce them. Thereupon he established officials. These having been established, it was necessary to have some one to unify them. So he set up a prince. Once a prince had been set up, the idea of honouring talent disappeared, and that of prizing honour arose. Thus in the highest antiquity, people loved their relatives and were fond of what was their own; in middle antiquity, they honoured talent and talked of moral virtue; and in later days, they prized honour and respected office. Honouring talent means vying with one another with doctrines, but setting up a prince means relegating talented men to unemployment. Loving one's relatives means making sefishness one's guiding principle, but the idea of equity and justice is to prevent selfishness from holding the field. But these three methods

did not aim at antagonistic purposes. The guiding principles of the
people are base, and they are not consistent in what they value. As
the conditions in the world change, different principles are practised. Therefore it is said that there is a fixed standard in a king's
principles. Indeed, a king's principles represent one viewpoint, and
those of a minister another. The principles each follows are different, but are one in both representing a fixed standard. Therefore, it
is said: 'When the people are stupid, by knowledge one may rise to
supremacy; when the world is wise, by force one may rise to
supremacy.' That means that when people are stupid, there are
plenty of strong men but not enough wise, and when the world
is wise, there are plenty of clever men, but not enough strong. It is
the nature of people, when they have no knowledge, to study; and
when they have no strength, to submit. So when Shen-nung taught
ploughing and attained supreme sway, the leadership was by means
of his knowledge; when T'ang and Wu made themselves strong and
attacked the feudal lords, the subjugation was by means of their
force. That is, in the case of uneducated people, when they possess
no knowledge, they are anxious to learn; in the case of an educated
society, not having force, it submits. Therefore, he who wishes to
attain supreme sway by means of love, rejects punishments, and he
who wishes to subjugate the feudal lords by means of force, relegates
virtue to the background. A sage does not imitate antiquity, nor
does he follow the present time. If he were to imitate antiquity, he
would be behind the times; and if he follows the present time, he is
obstructed by circumstances. The Chou dynasty did not imitate the
Shang dynasty, nor did the Hsia dynasty imitate the period of Yü;
the three dynasties encountered different circumstances, but all
three succeeded in attaining supremacy. So to rise to supremacy,
there is a definite way, but to hold it there are different principles.
For example, Wu as a rebel seized the empire, and yet he prized
obedience to the law; he disputed the empire, and yet exalted
compliancy; by force he seized it, but by righteousness he held it.
Nowadays strong countries aim at annexation, while weak countries
are concerned for defence by force, which means that compared
with early times they are not equal to the times of Yü and Hsia, and
compared with later times they do not practise the principles of
T'ang and Wu. Because the principles of T'ang and Wu are obstructed, of the countries of ten thousand chariots there is not one

that does not wage war, and of the countries of a thousand chariots there is not one that is not on the defence. These principles (of T'ang and Wu) have been obstructed a long time, and none of the rulers of the world is able to develop them. Therefore, there is not a fourth added to the three dynasties, and unless there be an intelligent ruler, there is none who succeeds in being obeyed. Now you want to develop the people by imitating the ancient rulers, but the people of old were simple through honesty, while the people of today are clever through artificiality. Wherefore, if you wish to imitate the ancients, you will have orderly government by promoting virtue, and if you wish to imitate modern times, you will have laws by emphasising punishments, and this is commonly distrusted. What the world now calls righteousness is the establishment of what people like and the abolishment of what they dislike, and what the world calls unrighteousness is the establishment of what people dislike and the abolishment of that in which they take delight.

The names and practice of these two methods may be inter-changed. It is necessary to examine this: if you establish what people delight in, then they will suffer from what they dislike; but if you establish what the people dislike, they will be happy in what they enjoy. How do I know that this is so? Because, if people are in sorrow, they think, and in thinking they invent various devices; Whereas if they enjoy themselves, they are dissolute, and dissol-uteness breeds idleness. Therefore, if you govern by punishment, the people will fear. Being fearful, they will not commit villainies; there being no villainies, people will be happy in what they enjoy. If, however, you teach the people by righteousness, then they will be lax, and if they are lax, there will be disorder; if there is disorder, the people will suffer from what they dislike. What I call profit is the basis of righteousness, but what the world calls righteousness is the way to violence. Indeed, in making the people correct, one always attains what they like by means of what they dislike, and one brings about what they dislike by means of what they like. In an orderly country, punishments are numerous and rewards rare. Therefore, in countries that attain supremacy, there is one reward to nine punish-ments, and in dismembered countries, nine rewards to every one punishment. Now, in proportion to the gravity or otherwise of the offence, there are light and heavy punishments, and in proportion to the greatness of the virtue, there are large or small rewards. These two differences are constantly applied in the world. If punishments are applied to accomplished crimes, then villainy will not be banished, and if rewards are bestowed for virtuous actions that have been achieved by the people, then offences will not cease. Now, if punishments cannot banish villainy, nor rewards put an end to offences, there will doubtless be disorder. Therefore, in the case of one who attains supremacy, punishments are applied at the intent to sin, so that great depravity cannot be bred; and rewards are bestowed on the denouncement of villainy, so that minor sins do not escape unnoticed. If, in governing a people, a condition can be brought about wherein great depravity cannot be bred and minor offences do not escape unnoticed, the state will be orderly, and being orderly, it is certain to be strong. If one country alone applies this method, there will be order only within its own borders; if two countries apply this method, the armies will have some rest; if the whole world applies this method, the highest state of virtue will be re-established. This is my way of reverting to virtue by death-penalties, and of making righteousness a corollary to violence.

Of old, people lived densely together and all dwelt in disorder, so they desired that there should be a ruler. However, why the empire was glad to have a ruler was because he would create order. Now, having rulers but no law, the evil is the same as if there were no rulers, and having laws that are not equal to the disorders is the same as if there were no law. The empire does not feel tranquil without a prince, but it takes pleasure in being stronger than the law, and thus the whole world is perturbed. Indeed, there is no greater benefit for the people in the empire than order, and there is no firmer order to be obtained than by establishing a prince; for establishing a prince, there is no more embracing method than making law supreme; for making law supreme, there is no more urgent task than banishing villainy, and for banishing villainy, there is no deeper basis than severe punishments. Therefore those who attain supremacy restrain by rewards and encourage by punishments, seek offences and not virtue, and rely on punishments in order to abolish punishments.

CHAPTER 3

8 The Unification of Words

When about to establish a state, it is necessary to examine standards and measures, to pay attention to law and order, to be vigilant in government duties, and to consolidate occupations with what is primary.[1] When standards and measures are regulated in accordance with the times, the customs of the country may be changed and the people will follow the standard regulations; if rules and laws are clear, the officials will commit no depravity; if the duties of the government are dealt with uniformly, the people will be available for use; if occupations with what is primary are consolidated, people will take pleasure in agriculture and will enjoy warfare. Now a sage, in establishing laws, alters the customs and causes the people to be engaged in agriculture, night and day. It is necessary to understand this. Indeed, people abide by their avocations and obey the regulations even to death, when the honorific titles which the ruler has instituted, and the rewards and penalties which he has established, are clear, and when, instead of employing sophists and intriguers, men of merit are set up. The result will be that the people will take pleasure in farming and enjoy warfare, because they see that the ruler honours farmers and soldiers, looks down upon sophists and artisans, and despises itinerant scholars. Therefore, when the people concentrate on one occupation, their families will be rich and their persons will be distinguished in the country; the ruler opens the way to public benefit and bars the gate of private intrigue, so that the people's strength is developed to the utmost. If toil in one's own interest does not gain distinction in the state, nor is admittance to the prince obtained through the gate of private intrigue, then under these circumstances, meritorious

1 i.e. agriculture and war.

ministers will be encouraged, and in consequence the orders of the ruler will be performed, waste lands will be opened up, dissolute people will disappear, and villainies will not sprout. He who, in administrating a country, is able to consolidate the people's strength and to make their occupation one, will be strong; he who is able to make the people attend to what is primary, and to prevent what is secondary,[2] is rich. A sage, in administrating a country, is able to consolidate its strength or to reduce it. When standards and measures are clear, then the people's strength is consolidated; if it is consolidated, but not developed, it cannot take effect. If it does take effect, but there are no riches, it will give rise to disorder. Therefore, for one who administers a country, the way to consolidate its strength is to make the country rich and its soldiers strong; the way to reduce the people's force is to attack the enemy and to encourage the people. If one only opens the way, without barring the gate, the short will grow long; when it has grown, and one does not attack, there will be villainy; if one debars without opening up, the people will be chaotic; if they are chaotic, and one does not make use of them, their strength will become great; if their strength is great, and one does not attack, there will be villainy and the parasites. So, consolidating their strength is brought about by unifying their occupation; reducing their force is brought about by attacking the enemy. In administrating a country, one should value the single-mindedness of the people; if they are single-minded, they are simple, and being simple, they farm; if they farm, they easily become diligent, and being diligent, they become rich. The rich should be despoiled of their riches by means of titles, so that they do not become dissolute. Those who are dissolute should be divested of their dissoluteness by punishments, so that they may concern themselves with agriculture. Therefore, if one is able only to consolidate force, and not to use it, disorder ensues; and one who is able only to reduce force, but not to consolidate it, will perish. So an intelligent ruler, who knows how to combine these two principles, will be strong, but that of one who does not know how to combine these two, will be dismembered.

Indeed, if a people are not orderly, it is because their prince follows inferior ways; and if the laws are not clear, it means that the

2 i.e. trade, etc.

prince causes disorder to grow. Therefore, an intelligent prince is one who does not follow an inferior way, nor causes disorder to grow; but he establishes himself by maintaining his authority, and creates order by giving laws; so that he gains possession of those who are treacherous towards their ruler; thus for all officials respectively rewards or penalties are fixed, so that employment will have a fixed standard. Under these circumstances, then, the country's regulations will be clear and the people's force will be used to the utmost; the titles granted by the ruler will be honoured and the . . . will be advanced.[3]

The rulers of the present day all desire to govern the people, but their way of helping them is disorderly – not because they take pleasure in disorder, but because they rest on antiquity and do not watch for the needs of the times; that is, the ruler models himself on antiquity, and as a result, is hampered by it; subordinates follow the present and do not change with the times, and when the changes in the customs of the world are not understood, and the conditions for governing the people are not examined, then the multiplication of rewards only leads to punishments, and the lightening of punishments only eliminates rewards.[4] Indeed, the ruler institutes punishments, but the people do not obey; his rewards are exhausted, but crimes continue to increase; for the people in their relation to the ruler think first of punishments and only afterwards of rewards. The sage's way, therefore, of organ-ising a country is not to imitate antiquity, nor to follow the present, but to govern in accordance with the needs of the times, and to make laws which take into account customs. For laws which are established without examining people's conditions do not succeed, but a government which is enacted fittingly for the times does not offend. Therefore, the government of the sage-kings examined attentively the people's occupations, and concentrated their attention on unifying them and on nothing else.

3 The text here is corrupt.
4 i.e. that the more rewards are promised, the more will people commit crimes, and the lighter the punishments are, the less people will strive for rewards.

9 Establishing Laws

I have heard that when the intelligent princes of antiquity established laws, the people were not wicked; when they undertook an enterprise, the required ability was practised spontaneously; when they distributed rewards, the army was strong. These three principles were the root of government. Indeed, why people were not wicked, when laws were established, was because the laws were clear and people profited by them; why the required ability was practised spontaneously, when an enterprise was undertaken, was because merits were clearly defined; and because these were clearly defined, the people exerted their forces; and this being so, the required ability was spontaneously practised; why the army was strong when rewards were distributed refers to titles and emoluments. Titles and emoluments are the goal of a soldier's ambition. Therefore, the principle on which princes distributed titles and emoluments was clear; when this was clear, the country became daily stronger, but when it was obscure, the country became daily weaker. Therefore, the principle on which titles and emoluments are distributed is the key to the state's preservation or ruin. The reason why a country is weak or a prince is ruined is not that there are no titles or emoluments, but that the principles followed therein are wrong. The principle followed by the Three Kings and the five Lords Protector was no other than that of giving titles and emoluments, and the reason that people emulated each other in merit was because the principles which they followed were clear. Thus the way in which intelligent princes utilised their ministers was that their employment was made dependent on the work which they had done, and rewards were bestowed on the merits which they had acquired. When the relation between merit and reward was clear, then the people emulated each other in merit. If, in administering a state, one succeeds in causing the people to exert their strength so that they emulate each other in merit, then the army will certainly be strong.

To be of the same rank as others and yet to stand to them in such relations as subject or concubine points to poverty or wealth; to be of the same territory as others and yet to be annexed by them points to strength or weakness; to have land, but the prince being in the one case strong and in the other weak, points to disorder or order. If there is a right method, even a territory of a square *li* is sufficient to give room to the body, and people may be attracted (to colonise); and if it but contains a market-place, riches may become many. Whoever has land cannot be called poor, and whoever has people cannot be called weak. If land is made truly productive, one need not be anxious about not being wealthy; if the people are truly employed, one need not fear force or violence; if virtue be clear and with the right teaching prevailing, one will succeed in utilising for oneself what the people have. Therefore, the intelligent kings utilised what was not their own, and employed those who were not their own subjects. The point to which intelligent kings attached importance was that of rewarding with titles only men of real merit; if this condition was fulfilled, honour and outer marks of distinction were awarded to them. If there were no honour connected with them, then people would not be anxious for noble rank, and if there were no outer marks of distinction, then people would not be concerned about titles. If titles are easily obtained, then people do not appreciate the highest titles nor the various other titles; if emoluments and rewards are not obtained through a definite gateway, people will not strive to the death for rank. For a prince there exists the fact that people have likes and dislikes; therefore, for it to be possible to govern the people, it is necessary that the prince should examine these likes and dislikes. Likes and dislikes are the basis of rewards and punishments. Now, the nature of man is to like titles and emoluments and to dislike punishments and penalties. A prince institutes these two in order to guide men's wills, and he establishes what they desire. Now, if titles follow upon the people's exertion of strength, if rewards follow upon their acquisition of merit, and if the prince succeeds in making people believe in this as firmly as they do in the shining of sun and moon, then his army will have no equal. Among the princes of men there are some who bestow titles, but whose army is weak; there are some who grant emoluments, but whose state is poor; there are some who have fixed laws, but who yet suffer disorder. These three things are calamities for a country. For if a ruler of men places the making easy of audiences before the acquiring of merit, then although he bestows titles, his army will be weak; if people, without risking their lives in dangers, can obtain profit and emoluments, then the granting of emoluments will only make the country poor. If the law has neither measures nor figures, then affairs will daily become more complicated, and although laws have been established, yet the result will be that the administration will be in disorder. Therefore, an intelligent prince, in directing his people, will so direct them that they will exert their strength to the utmost in order to strive for a particular merit; and if, when they have acquired merit, riches and honour follow upon it, there will be no bravery in private causes. Therefore, if this teaching spreads and becomes successful, then when that is the case, ministers will be loyal, princes intelligent, order manifest, and the army strong. Therefore, in general, an intelligent prince in his administration relies on force and not on virtue, and thus, without his being anxious or fatigued, merit will be established. When measures and figures have been instituted, law can be followed. Therefore, it is necessary that a ruler of men should pay attention to himself.

Indeed, Li Chu saw an autumn's hair at a distance of more than a hundred paces, but he could not transfer his sharp vision to others; Wu Huo was able to lift a weight of a thousand *chün*, but could not transfer his great strength to others; and indeed sages cannot transfer to others the personality and nature that is inherent in them.

But that whereby success may be attained – that is the law.

10 The Method of Warfare

Generally in the method of warfare, the fundamental principle consists in making government measures supremely prevalent. If this is done, then the people concerned will have no disputes; and having no disputes, they will have no thought of self-interest, but will have the interest of the ruler in mind. Therefore a real king, through his measures, will cause people to be fearful in fights between various cities, but brave in wars against external foes. If people have been trained to attack dangers with energy, they will, as a result, think lightly of death. Should the enemy be routed as soon as the engagement has begun, and should he not stop in his rout abstain from further pursuit. Therefore does the *The Art of War* say:[1] 'In a big battle, in the event of victory, pursue the fugitives not further than 10 *li*; in a small battle, in the event of victory, pursue the fugitives not further than 5 *li*.' When hostilities begin, weigh the strength[2] of the enemy; if your organisation is not equal to his, do not engage him in battle; if your provisions are not equal to his, do not protract the war; if the enemy is numerically strong, do not invade his territory;[3] if the enemy is in every way your inferior, attack him without hesitation. Therefore it is said: 'The great rule of an army is prudence.' By estimating the strength of the enemy and by examining one's own hosts, victory or defeat may be known beforehand.[4]

1 I do not find this in Sun Tzu's *Art of War*, but the meaning resembles his dictum: 'Do not press a desperate foe too hard.' (ch. 8).
2 cf. Sun Tzu, ch. 4. 'In respect of military method, we have: (1) measurement, (2) estimation of quantity, (3) calculation, (4) balancing of chances, (5) victory.'
3 cf. Sun Tzu ch. 9. 'The principles to be observed by an invading force', and passim.
4 cf. Sun Tzu ch. 3. 'Hence the saying: "If you know the enemy and know yourself, you need not fear the result of a hundred battles. If you know yourself but not the enemy, for every victory gained, you will also suffer a defeat. If you know neither the enemy nor yourself, you will run risks in every battle." '

The army of a real king does not boast of victory, nor does it harbour rancour for defeat. That it does not boast of victory is because it ascribes it to its clever tactics;[5] that it does not harbour rancour for defeat is because it knows why it has failed. If the relative strength of the armies is well-matched, the side that has clever leadership will win, and the side that has inferior leadership will lose. If the organisation has its origin in the calculations made in the temple,[6] then it will win, whether the leadership is clever or inferior. He who holds victorious tactics will be so strong that he will attain supremacy. If people are submissive and obey their ruler, then the country will become rich and the army victorious; and if this state of affairs is maintained for long, he will surely attain supremacy.

But it is a mistake for an army to penetrate deeply into the enemy's country, in difficult and unsurmountable terrain and cut off in a cul-de-sac; the men will become exhausted, hungry and thirsty as well, and will, moreover, fall victims to disease. This is the way to defeat. Therefore he who intends to direct the people . . . and he who mounts a good horse cannot but be on his guard.[7]

---

5 And not to individual merit.

6 i.e. before the battle. Cf. Sun Tzu, ch. 1. 'Indeed, if a general, after having made his calculations in the temple before the battle, is victorious, it is because a great many of his calculations have come true. But, if, after having made his calculations in the temple before the battle, he is not victorious, it is because only a few of his calculations have come true. Thus do many calculations lead to victory and few calculations to defeat. How much more no calculations at all! Looking at it from this point of view, one can see who will gain victory or suffer defeat.'

7 The text is corrupt her.

11 The Establishment of Fundamentals

Generally, in the utilising of soldiers, there are three stages to victory: prior to the outbreak of hostilities, laws should be fixed; laws being fixed, they should become the custom; when they have become customary, supplies should be provided. These three things should be done within the country before the soldiers can be sent abroad. For performing these three things, there are two conditions; the first is to support the law, so that it can be applied; the second is to obtain the right men in appointments, so that the law can be established. For reliance on masses is said to be the assembling of a mob; reliance on outward appearances is said to be smartness; reliance on fame and sight is said to be deceitfulness. If one relies on any one of these three, one's soldiers may be captured. Therefore is it said: 'The strong are unbending; they fight for what they desire. By fighting, their strength develops to the full, and thus they are prepared. In this way, they have no rival in the four seas, and by order prevailing, products are accumulated; by the accumulation of products, it is possible for the rewards to be big.' If rewards are uniform, rank will be honoured; if rank is honoured, rewards will bring profit. Therefore is it said: 'The army being based on a state of order, there is a marvellous result; custom being based on law, ten thousand changes of circumstances are brought about; a condition of supremacy being based upon the mind, it is outwardly manifested in a condition of preparedness. If these three points of view are all taken into consideration, the result will be that the strong may be firmly established.' Thus orderly government is the necessary result of strength, and strength again of orderly government; orderly government of riches, and riches again of orderly government; riches of strength, and strength again of riches. Therefore is it said: 'The way to orderly government and strength is to discuss fundamentals.'

12 Military Defence

A state that has to fight on four fronts values defence, and a state that rests against the sea values attack. For, if a state that fights on four fronts is fond of raising soldiers, it will be in a dangerous position, as it has to resist four neighbours. As soon as a country with four neighbours begins hostilities, four countries mobilise armies; therefore is it said that the country is in a dangerous position. If a state that has to fight on four fronts is unable to raise, from a city of ten thousand houses, an army of more than ten thousand men, then the state will be in a dangerous position. Therefore is it said: 'A state that has to fight on four fronts should concern itself with defensive warfare.' In defending walled cities, the best way is, with the strength of the worn-out men, to fight the fresh strength of the invaders. It is assaults upon walled cities that wear out the strength of men. So long as the walled cities have not all been razed, the invaders have no means of penetrating the country. This is meant by the saying that the strength of worn-out men should fight the fresh strength of the invading force. But when the walled cities have all been razed and the foreign army thus finds the means of penetrating, then certainly it will be exhausted, and the people within the country will be rested. Fighting with rested strength against those of exhausted strength is said to be fighting with the strength of fresh men against the worn-out strength of the invading forces. All these are called the misfortunes attendant upon the besieging of walled cities. It is regarded as a misfortune that always, in capturing cities, the strength of the army is worn out. In these three things misfortune is due, not to insufficient effort, but to mistaken generalship.

The way to hold a city is to have abundant strength. Therefore is it said: 'When the invading force musters its levies, mobilise as many as three armies, and divide them according to the number of the chariots of the invading force.' Of these three armies, one should be formed of able-bodied men, one of able-bodied women, and one of the old and feeble men and women. These are called the three armies. Cause the army of able-bodied men, with abundant provisions and sharp weapons, to marshal themselves and to await the enemy; cause the able-bodied women, with abundant provisions and ramparts at their backs, to marshal themselves and to await orders, so as to make, at the approach of the invaders, earthworks as an obstruction, and traps, chevaux-de-frise and pitfalls, to pull down the supporting beams and to tear down the houses, to transport what is transportable, and to burn what is untransportable, so that the invaders are not able to make use thereof in their attack. Cause the army of the old and feeble to guard the oxen, horses, sheep and swine, and to collect all that is consumable of plants and water, to feed them therewith, so as to obtain food for the able-bodied men and women. But see to it carefully that the three armies do not intermingle. If the able-bodied men mingle with the army of the able-bodied women, they will attach great value to the safety of the women, and wicked people will have opportunities for intrigue, with the result that the state will perish. Taking pleasure in the women's company, the men will be afraid of disturbing reports and so not even the brave will fight. If the able-bodied men and women intermingle with the army of the old and feeble, then the old will arouse the compassion of the able-bodied, and the feeble the pity of the strong. Compassion and pity in the heart cause brave people to be more anxious and fearful people not to fight. Therefore is it said: 'See to it carefully that the three armies do not intermingle.' This is the way to have abundant strength.

13 Making Orders Strict

If orders are made strict, orderly government is not delayed, and if laws are equable, officials are not wicked. Once the law is fixed, one should not damage it with virtuous words; if men of merit are appointed to office, people will have little to say; but if men of virtue are appointed to office, people will have much to say. The practice of good government begins with making judgments. Where five hamlets are the unit for judgments, supremacy is attained; where ten hamlets are the unit for judgments, there is merely strength. He who procrastinates in creating order will be dismembered. Govern by punishments and wage war by rewards; seek transgressors and do not seek the virtuous. Therefore, if the law is fixed and not altered, then . . . [1] If in the country there are no wicked people, there is no wicked trade in the capital. If affairs are many and secondary things are numerous, if agriculture is relaxed and criminals gain the upper hand, then the country will certainly be dismembered.

If the people have a surplus of grain, cause them to obtain office and rank by means of their cereals; if through their own efforts they can count upon obtaining office and rank, farmers will not be lazy.

If a tube of no more than four inches has no bottom, it can certainly not be filled; to confer office, to give rank and to grant salaries, without regard to merit, is like having no bottom.

If a state, when poor, applies itself to war, the poison will originate on the enemy's side, and it will not have the six parasites, but will certainly be strong. If a state, when rich, does not apply itself to war, the poison is transferred to its own interior, and it will have the six kinds of parasites and will certainly be weak. If the state confers office and gives rank according to merit, it may be said to be planning with complete wisdom, and fighting with complete courage. Such a country will certainly have no equal. If a state

1 The text is corrupt.

confers office and gives rank according to merit, then government measures will be simple and words will be few. This may be said to be abolishing laws by means of the law and abolishing words by means of words. But if a state confers office and gives rank according to the six parasites, then government measures will be complicated and words will arise. This may be said to be bringing about laws by means of the law and causing volubility by means of words. Then the prince will devote himself to talking, officials will be distracted with ruling the wicked, wicked officials will gain their own way, and those who have merit will daily retire more. This may be said to be failure. When one has to observe ten rules, there is confusion: when one has only one to observe, there is order. When the law is fixed, then those who are fond of practising the six parasites perish. If people occupy themselves entirely with agriculture, the state is rich; if the six parasites are not practised, then soldiers and people will, without exception, vie with one another for encouragement and will be glad to be employed by their ruler; the people within the borders will vie with one another to regard it as glorious, and none will regard it as disgraceful. Following upon this comes the condition where people will do it because they are encouraged by means of rewards and restrained by means of punishment. But the worst case is when people hate it, are anxious about it, and are ashamed of it; then they adorn their outer appearances and are engaged in talking; they are ashamed of taking a position and exalt culture. In this way they shun agriculture and war, and outside interests being thus furnished, it will be a perilous position for the country. To have people dying of hunger and cold, and to have unwillingness to fight for the sake of profit and emolument, are usual occurrences in a perishing state. The six parasites are: rites and music, odes and history, moral culture and virtue, filial piety and brotherly love, sincerity and faith, chastity and integrity, benevolence and righteousness, criticism of the army and being ashamed of fighting. If there are these twelve things, the ruler is unable to make people farm and fight, and then the state will be so poor that it will be dismembered.[2] If

2 cf. section 3, section 4, section 5, section 17. The numbers given are different in each case; here there are really sixteen things.

these twelve things come together, then it may be said that the prince's administration is not stronger than his ministers and that the administration of his officials is not stronger than his people.[3] This is said to be a condition where the six parasites are stronger than the government. When these twelve gain an attachment,[4] then dismemberment ensues. Therefore to make a country prosperous, these twelve things should not be practised; then the state will have much strength, and no one in the empire will be able to invade it. When its soldiers march out, they will capture their objective, and having captured it, will be able to hold it. When it keeps its soldiers in reserve and does not attack, it will certainly become rich. The court officials do not reject any merits, however few they may be, nor do they detract from any merits, however many they may be. Office and rank are obtained according to the acquired merit, and even though there may be sophistical talk, it will be impossible thereby to obtain undue precedence. This is said to be government by statistics. In attacking with force, ten points are gained for every one point undertaken, but in attacking with words, a hundred are lost for every one marched out. If a state loves force, it is said to attack with what is difficult; if a state loves words, it is said to attack with what is easy. If penalties are heavy and rewards few, then the ruler loves his people and they will die for him; if rewards are heavy and penalties light, then the ruler does not love his people nor will they die for him.

If the profit disappears through one outlet only, the state will have no equal; if it disappear through two outlets, the state will have only half the profit; but if the profit disappears through ten outlets, the state will not be preserved. If heavy penalties are clear, there will be great control, but if they are not clear, there will be the six parasites. If the six kinds of parasites come together, then the people are not fit for employment. Therefore, in a prosperous country, when punishments are applied, the people will be closely associated with the ruler, and when rewards are applied they will reap profit.

In applying punishments, light offences should be punished heavily; if light offences do not appear, heavy offence will not

3 cf. section 5, and section 7.
4 cf. section 4, and section 20.

come. This is said to be abolishing penalties by means of penalties, and if penalties are abolished, affairs will succeed. If crimes are serious and penalties light, penalties will appear and trouble will arise. This is said to be bringing about penalties by means of penalties, and such a state will surely be dismembered.

A sage prince understands what is essential in affairs, and therefore in his administration of the people there is that which is most essential. For the fact that uniformity in the manipulating of rewards and punishments supports moral virtue, is connected with human psychology. A sage-prince, by his ruling of men, is certain to win their hearts; consequently he is able to use force. Force produces strength, strength produces prestige, prestige produces virtue; and so virtue has its origin in force, which a sage-prince alone possesses, and therefore he is able to transmit benevolence and righteousness to the empire.

14 The Cultivation of the Right Standard

Orderly government is brought about in a state by three things. The first is law, the second good faith, and the third right standards. Law is exercised in common by the prince and his ministers. Good faith is established in common by the prince and his ministers. The right standard is fixed by the prince alone. If a ruler of men fails to observe it, there is danger; if prince and ministers neglect the law and act according to their own self-interest, disorder is the inevitable result. Therefore if law is established, rights and duties are made clear, and self-interest does not harm the law, then there is orderly government. If the fixing of the right standard is decided by the prince alone, there is prestige. If the people have faith in his rewards, then their activities will achieve results; and if they have faith in his penalties, then wickedness will have no starting point. Only an intelligent ruler loves right standards and values good faith, and will not, for the sake of self-interest, harm the law. For if he speaks many liberal words but cuts down his rewards, then his subjects will not be of service; and if he issues one severe order after another, but does not apply the penalties, people will despise the death-penalty.

In general, rewards are a civil measure and penalties a military. Civil and military measures are the summary of the law. Therefore an intelligent ruler places reliance on the law; [an intelligent ruler], if things are not kept hidden from him, is called intelligent, and if he is not deceived, is called perspicacious. Therefore he benefits by giving liberal rewards; and by making penalties severe, he ensures that he is feared. He does not neglect those that are distant, nor does he run counter to those that are near. Thus ministers will not hide things from their ruler, nor will inferiors deceive their superiors. Those who are engaged in governing, in the world, chiefly dismiss the law and place reliance on private appraisal, and this is what brings disorder in a state. The early kings hung up scales with standard weights, and fixed the length of feet and inches, and to the present day these are followed as models because their divisions were clear. Now dismissing standard scales and yet deciding weight, or abolishing feet and inches and yet forming an opinion about length – even an intelligent merchant would not apply this system, because it would lack definiteness. Now, if the back is turned on models and measures, and reliance is placed on private appraisal, in all those cases there would be a lack of definiteness. Only a Yao would be able to judge knowledge and ability, worth or unworth, without a model. But the world does not consist exclusively of Yaos! Therefore, the ancient kings understood that no reliance should be placed on individual opinions or biased approval, so they set up models and made the distinctions clear. Those who fulfilled the standard were rewarded, those who harmed the public interest were punished. The standards for rewards and punishments were not wrong in their appraisals, and therefore people did not dispute them. But if the bestowal of office and the granting of rank are not carried out according to the labour borne, then loyal ministers have no advancement; and if in awarding rewards and giving emoluments the respective merits are not weighed, then fighting soldiers will not enter his service.

Generally, the principle on which ministers serve their prince are dependent, in most cases, on what the ruler likes. If the ruler likes law, then the ministers will make law their principle in serving; if the prince likes words, then the ministers will make words their principle in serving. If the prince likes law, then upright scholars will come to the front, but if he likes words, then ministers full of praise for some and blame for others will be at his side. If public and private interests are clearly distinguished, then even small-minded men do not hate men of worth, nor do worthless men envy those of merit. For when Yao and Shun established their rule over the empire, they did not keep the benefits of the empire for themselves, but it was for the sake of the empire that they established their rule. In making the imperial succession dependent on worth and ability, they did not intend to alienate fathers and sons from one another, and to conciliate distant people,[1] but they did it because they had a true insight into the ways of order and disorder.

1 This is a reference to the fact that Yao and Shun did not give the empire to their sons. (Yao and Shun are legendary sages and emperors.)

So, too, the Three Kings conciliated people by righteousness, and the five Lords Protector rectified the feudal lords by law; that is, in all these cases, none took for himself the benefits of the empire. They ruled for the sake of the empire, and thus, when those who held positions had corresponding merit, the empire enjoyed their administration and no one could harm it.

But, nowadays, princes and ministers of a disorderly world each, on a small scale, appropriates the profits of his own state, and each exercises the burden of his own office, for his private benefit. This is why the states are in a perilous position. For the relation between public and private interests is what determines existence or ruin.

However, if models and measures are abolished and private appraisal is favoured, then bad ministers will let their standards be influenced by money, in order to obtain emoluments, and officials of the various ranks will, in a stealthy and hidden manner, make extortions from the people. The saying runs: 'Many woodworms and the wood snaps, a large fissure and the wall collapses.' So if ministers of state vie with one another in selfishness and do not heed the people, then inferiors are estranged from superiors. When this happens, there is a fissure in the state. If the officials of the various ranks make extortions from the people, stealthily and in a hidden manner, they are for the people like woodworms. Therefore is it exceptional in the world that where there are fissures and woodworms, ruin does not follow. That is why intelligent kings placed reliance on the law and removed self-interest, so that the state should have no fissures and no woodworms.

CHAPTER 4

15 The Encouragement of Immigration

In a territory of a hundred square *li*, a tenth should be occupied by mountains and hills, a tenth by glades and morasses, a tenth by valleys, dales, and running water, a tenth by cities, towns, and highways, a tenth by barren fields, and four-tenths by fertile fields.[1] In this way 50,000 workmen can be fed; those mountains and hills, glades and morasses, valleys and dales, are able to provide the required material, and the cities, towns and highways are sufficient to accommodate the people concerned. This was the proportion according to which the early kings regulated the land and divided the people. Now, the territory of Ch'in comprises five times a thousand square *li*,[2] but the soil fit for growing corn cannot occupy more than two-fifths. The area of the fields does not come up to a million *mu*, and the produce and treasures of its glades and morasses, of its valleys and dales, and of its famous mountains and big rivers, are also incompletely utilised. This means that the population is ill-proportioned to the territory. The neighbours of Ch'in are the three Chin states,[3] and of these Han and Wei are fond of employing soldiers. Their territory is narrow, but their population is numerous; their dwellings are built higgledy-piggledy, and they live close together; their grain production is small, and merchants charge interest.

The people on the one hand do not have their names registered,[4] and on the other hand have no fields or houses, so that for

1 One-tenth is lacking.

2 1,000 *li* is the standard of a big country.

3 The three states, Han, Wei, and Chao, into which the state of Chin had been divided in 376 BC.

4 i.e. for soldiering

subsistence they rely on evil occupations and pursuits of minor importance,[5] with the result that those who are exempt from taxation because they live in steep and inaccessible places, in morasses and by streams, are more than a half of the population. Therefore, it would appear that a condition where the territory is not sufficient to support the population is still worse than that where, as in the case of Ch'in, the population is insufficient to fill the territory.

In reflecting upon the nature of the people, what they desire are fields and houses. Now, whereas it is probable that these are what Chin does not have, it is beyond doubt that Ch'in has them in surplus. If, this being so, people nevertheless do not come west, it is because the soldiers of Ch'in are in sad plight and the people suffer hardships. I venture to think that the intelligence of Your Majesty's[6] officials takes a mistaken view: that is, the reason why we remain weak, and do not succeed in enticing the people of the three Chin states, is that we are sparing in granting titles and regard the exemption from taxes as a serious matter. They argue as follows: 'The three Chin states are weak because their people are concerned with pleasure and because exemptions and rank are treated lightly. Ch'in, on the other hand, is strong because its people are concerned with hard work, and exemptions and the conferment of rank are treated seriously; should we now confer many titles and grant exemptions from taxation for long periods, then we should be letting go of the principle by which Ch'in has become strong and should be doing exactly that which has made the Chin states weak.' This is the argument that causes Your Majesty's officials to regard the conferring of titles as a serious matter, and to be sparing in the granting of exemptions from taxation.

I venture, however, to think that this is wrong. The object in causing the people hardship and in strengthening the army is to attack the enemy and to realise one's desires. *The Art of War* says:[7] 'If the enemy is weak, the army is strong.' This expression means

5 i.e. trade

6 A title which the rulers of Ch'in adopted in 325 BC, i.e. after the death of Shang Yang.

7 cf. section 10, for other quotations.

that one does not fail in attack, but the enemy fails in defence. Now for four generations the Chin states have gained no victory over Ch'in. Since the time of King Hsiang of Wei,[8] the times that the three Chin states have been defeated by Ch'in, in small or big battles, in open battle or in storming defended cities, have been innumerable. The reason that in spite of this they do not submit to Ch'in is that Ch'in has been able to conquer their territory, but unable to captivate their people.

Now, if Your Majesty will issue a favourable proclamation to the effect that those soldiers of the various feudal lords who will come and submit, will be granted exemption for three generations, without hearing anything of military affairs, and that those who live within the four boundaries of Ch'in, in the mountains and on the slopes, on hills and in marshes, will not be called upon for ten years for military service, and if this is made clear in the law, it will be possible to create a million workers. I have said before: 'In reflecting upon the nature of the people, what they desire are fields and houses. Now, whereas it is probable that Chin does not have these, it is certain that Ch'in has them in surplus. If in spite of this the people do not migrate westward, it is because the soldiers of Ch'in are in sore plight, and the people suffer hardships.' Now, if they are benefited with land and houses, and exemption from taxes for three generations is granted them – that is, if a point is made of giving them what they desire, and of not causing them to perform what they dislike – then all the people from east of the mountains will migrate westward.

Moreover, to state the case frankly: if You do not act thus, You may fill the empty and waste lands and produce natural wealth, so that a million people are engaged in the fundamental occupation,[9] and the benefits will be manifold, but how will You prevent the soldiers from failing in their attacks? Indeed, the trouble with Ch'in is, on the one hand, that if it raises soldiers and wages war, the country is poor, and on the other hand, if it remains quiet and

8 334–319 BC, but the same person reigned from 370–335 as Duke Hui-ch'eng. Again the events mentioned occurred long after the death of Shang Yang, and the 'four generations' which are mentioned enable us to date this paragraph as being approximately of the middle of the third century BC.
9 i.e. agriculture.

farms, the enemy obtains respite. Your Majesty cannot combine success in these two fields. So, although for three generations[10] it has waged successful wars, yet it has not subjected the empire. Now, if the old population of Ch'in are engaged in warfare, and if the newcomers are caused to occupy themselves with agriculture, then even though the army may stay a hundred days outside the frontier, within the borders not a moment will be lost for agriculture. Thus You may be successful both in enriching and in becoming strong.

When I speak of soldiers, I do not mean that all should be raised and mobilised to the last man, but according to the number of armies, soldiers, chariots and cavalry that can be furnished within the territory, cause the old population of Ch'in to serve as soldiers and the new people to provide fodder and food. Should there be a state in the empire that does not submit, then Your Majesty should, herewith, in spring prevent their farming, in summer live on their produce, in autumn lay hold of their harvest, and in winter pickle their vegetables: by the methods of the 'Great Warfare' shake their fundamental means of existence, and by those of the 'Extensive Culture' pacify their descendants. If Your Majesty follows this policy, then within ten years the various feudal lords will have no people from other countries,[11] and wherefore then should Your Majesty be sparing in the conferment of titles or regard exemption from taxes as a serious matter? At the victories in the Chou[12] and in the Hua[13] battles, Ch'in extended its territory eastwards by cutting off heads, but it is clear that there was no advantage in this eastward extension; and yet officials regard these events as great accomplishments, because loss was

10 cf. above, 'four generations'.

11 These will all emigrate to Ch'in.

12 In 771 BC, when Duke Hsiang of Ch'in assisted the Chou dynasty against the Jung barbarians and escorted King P'ing to his new capital in Lo as a reward, he became an independent feudal lord, and so laid the foundation of Ch'in.

13 In 697 BC, Duke Wu fought the P'eng-hsi tribe who cut Ch'in off from the Chou, and made his way to the Hua Mountain. This mountain lies a little to the south of the sub-prefecture of Hua-yin in the prefecture of T'ung-chou in the present Shensi.

inflicted on the enemy. Now, if the people of the three Chin states are induced to immigrate by means of grasslands and cottages, and if they are made to occupy themselves with primary things, then this way of inflicting damage on the enemy is just as real as a victory in war, and Ch'in will have the advantage of obtaining agricultural products. Conversely, by this plan, two birds will be hit with one stone. Further, in the victories in the Chou and Hua battles, or in that at Ch'ang-p'ing,[14] how many people did Ch'in lose, and how many soldiers, both of the people and of the foreign inhabitants, were unable to occupy themselves with primary affairs? I venture to think that they were innumerable. Suppose amongst Your Majesty's ministers there should be one able, with a half of these losses, to weaken Chin and to strengthen Ch'in as much as by the victories in these three battles, then would Your Majesty, no doubt, grant him big rewards. Now, by the method which I propose, the people would not have a single day's scutage nor would the officials have the expense of great sums of money, while Chin would be weakened and Ch'in strengthened more than by three battles; but if Your Majesty still does not approve, then Your servant is too stupid to understand it.'

Amongst the citizens of Ch'i was one Tung-kuo Ch'ang, who had very many desires and wished to have ten thousand pieces of gold. When his retainer begged for a monetary subsidy (in case he would obtain that money), he would not give it, saying: 'I want to use it to obtain a fief.' His retainer became angry, and left him and went to Sung, saying: 'This is being stingy about what he has not; therefore he is now in a worse position than when he first had me with him.'[15] Now Chin has the people, and Ch'in is sparing in the granting of exemptions from taxes; this is being stingy about what one has not, with the result that one loses what one might have. Is this not just like Tung-kuo Ch'ang's being stingy about what he did not have, and so losing his retainer?[16]

14 In 260 BC, Ch'in completely routed the army of Chao at Ch'ang-p'ing. The reference to this battle here is of particular interest, as it shows that this part of the text, at any rate, is about a century later than Shang Yang himself. The words here may be a later addition, as a few lines earlier only two, and not three, battles are mentioned.

15 Because the retainer had left him.

16 'A bird in the hand is worth two in the bush.'

Moreover, in antiquity, there were Yao and Shun, who in their lifetime were praised; in the middle ages there were T'ang and Wu, during whose reigns people submitted. These are the three[17] Kings, who are praised by ten thousand generations and are regarded as sage-kings. Yet their methods cannot be applied in later times. Should You now make exemptions from taxation for three generations, You would he able completely to subject the three Chin states. This is not, like the virtuous kings, merely establishing the present times, . . . [18] but effecting that later generations shall be at the service of the king![19] This, however, does not mean that I do not welcome a sage, but it is difficult to await a sage.

17 Should be four.
18 There may be an omission in the text here.
19 The idea is that the kings of antiquity only made the country strong during their own reigns, but by this suggested far-sighted policy, the results would chiefly appear later.

16 Compendium of Penalties

(Lost)

17 Rewards and Punishments

The way in which a sage administers a state is by unifying rewards, unifying punishments, and unifying education. The effect of unifying rewards is that the army will have no equal; the effect of unifying punishments is that orders will be carried out; the effect of unifying education is that inferiors will obey superiors. Now if one understands rewards, there should be no expense; if one understands punishments, there should be no death penalty; if one understands education, there should be no changes, and so people would know the business of the people and there would be no divergent customs. The climax in the understanding of rewards is to bring about a condition of having no rewards; the climax in the understanding of punishments is to bring about a condition of having no punishments; the climax in the understanding of education is to bring about a condition of having no education.

What I mean by the unifying of rewards is that profits and emoluments, office and rank, should be determined exclusively by military merit, and that there should not be different reasons for distributing them. For thus the intelligent and the stupid, the noble and the humble, the brave and the timorous, the virtuous and the worthless, will all apply to the full whatever knowledge they may have in their breasts, exert to the uttermost whatever strength they may have in their limbs, and will be at the service of their ruler even to death; and the outstanding heroes, the virtuous and the good, of the whole empire will follow him, like flowing water, with the result that the army will have no equal, and commands will be carried out throughout the whole empire. A country of ten thousand chariots will not dare to assemble its soldiers in the plains of the Middle Kingdom; nor will a country of a thousand chariots dare to defend a walled city. Should a country of ten thousand chariots assemble its soldiers in the plains of the Middle Kingdom, one would rout its army in battle; and should a country of a thousand chariots defend a walled city, one would in the assault, capture that town. If, in battles, one always routs the other's army and, in assaults, one always captures the other's towns, with the result that finally one has all the cities, and all their riches accrue, then what expense or loss can one suffer, even though there are rich congratulatory rewards?

In days of old, T'ang was invested with Tsan-mao,[1] Wen-wang was invested with Ch'i-chou,[2] a district of a hundred square *li*, T'ang fought a battle with Chieh in the fields of Ming-t'iao,[3] Wu-wang fought a battle with Chou in the fields of Mu,[4] and utterly defeated the 'nine armies',[5] and finally split up the land and gave fiefs to the feudal lords. The officers and soldiers who retired from the ranks all received land, with the peasants belonging to it, in hamlets of 25 families;[6] the chariots were given a rest, and were no longer mounted; the horses were set at liberty on the southern slopes of Mount Hua; the oxen were set at liberty in the meadows, and they were allowed to grow old without being reassembled (for war). This was the way of T'ang and Wu of giving rewards. Therefore is it said: 'If all the people in the empire had had to be

1 Tsan-mao is said to have been to the south of the present prefecture of Shang-ch'iu in Honan province.

2 The town of Chou, at the foot of the Ch'i mountains (the prefecture Feng-hsiang in Shansi province) was the home of the later Chou dynasty.

3 Ming-t'iao was the name of a steep hill in the sub-prefecture of An-i, in Shensi province.

4 Mu, south of the sub-prefecture of Chi, prefecture of Wei-hui, in Honan province.

5 The expression 'nine armies' is used of the Imperial Army.

6 King Chao of Ch'u wanted to present Confucius with 700 hamlets with their 'god of the soil', and the peasants attached to it, and of Kuan-tzû it is said that he had received 300 'registered gods of the soil' which made him the richest man in Ch'i. This, however, did not constitute a fief, but the land with its tenants was given rather in usufruct. In the primitive organisation of twenty-five families, each *li* had its own 'god of the soil'.

rewarded with the produce of Tsan-mao and Ch'i-chou, no one would have received a pint, and if all the people of the empire had had to be rewarded with its money, no one would have received a cash.' Therefore is it said: 'If a prince of a territory of a hundred *li* invests his ministers with fiefs, he greatly increases his original territory.' How is it that the rewards received, beginning with those to officers and soldiers retired from the ranks, which consisted of land, with the peasants belonging to it, in hamlets of 25 families, were even more liberal than those to horses and oxen? Because they (those kings) knew well how to reward the people of the empire according to the possessions of the empire. Therefore do I say: 'If one understands rewards there is no expense.' Since T'ang and Wu destroyed Chieh[7] and Chou,[8] no harm was done within the four seas, and the empire enjoyed great stability; the five storehouses were constructed, the five weapons were stored away, military affairs were set aside, culture and education were practised, shields and spears were carried reversed, writing tablets were stuck in the girdle,[9] and music was performed in order to manifest one's virtue – such a condition of affairs prevailed in those times. Rewards and emoluments were not bestowed and yet the people were orderly. Therefore I say: 'The climax in the understanding of rewards is to bring about a condition where there are no longer rewards.'

What I mean by the unification of punishments is that punishments should know no degree or grade, but that from ministers of state and generals down to great officers and ordinary folk, whosoever does not obey the king's commands, violates the interdicts of the state, or rebels against the statutes fixed by the ruler, should be guilty of death and should not be pardoned.[10] Merit acquired in the past should not cause a decrease in the punishment for demerit later, nor should good behaviour in the past cause any derogation

---

7 The last emperor of the Hsia dynasty.

8 The last emperor of the Yin dynasty.

9 This tablet is amongst the appurtenances carried about his person by an accomplished young gentleman.

10 The tradition of Shang Yang's life shows that in this point he acted according to his own reported teaching, and even expected the crown prince to obey the law.

of the law for wrong done later. If loyal ministers and filial sons do
wrong, they should be judged according to the full measure of
their guilt, and if amongst the officials who have to maintain the
law and to uphold an office, there are those who do not carry out
the king's law, they are guilty of death and should not be pardoned,
but their punishment should be extended to their family for three
generations. Colleagues who, knowing their offence, inform their
superiors will themselves escape punishment. In neither high nor
low offices should there be an automatic hereditary succession to
the office, rank, lands or emoluments of officials. Therefore do I
say that if there are severe penalties that extend to the whole
family, people will not dare to try (how far they can go), and as
they dare not try, no punishments will be necessary. The former
kings, in making their interdicts, did not put to death, or cut off
people's feet, or brand people's faces, because they sought to harm
those people, but with the object of prohibiting wickedness and
stopping crime; for there is no better means of prohibiting wickedness and stopping crime than by making punishments heavy. If
punishments are heavy and rigorously applied, then people will not
dare to try (how far they can go), with the result that, in the state,
there will be no people punished. Because there are no people
punished in the state, I say that if one understands punishments,
there is no capital punishment.

Duke Wen of Chin[11] wished to make clear the system of
punishments, in order to gain the affection of the people. Thereupon, he assembled together all the feudal lords and great officers
in the Shih-ch'ien Palace, but Tien Hsieh arrived too late and
asked for punishment.[12] The prince said: 'Employ stabbing', and
the lictors thereupon cut through Tien Hsieh's spine and made
him die an expiatory death. The scholars of the state of Chin,
having investigated the matter, were all afraid, and said: 'Considering that Tien Hsieh was a favourite and still he has been sawn
through, as an expiatory death, how will it fare with us?' He raised
an army and attacked Ts'ao and Wu-lu. He also overturned the

12 According to the laws of the Chou dynasty, Chou-li, ch. 18, p. 24b, at
military inspections, a late arrival was punished with death.

lowlands of Cheng and veered towards the east the fields of Wei; he conquered the people of Ching at Ch'eng-p'u.[13] The soldiers of his three armies were so disciplined that stopping them was as if their feet were cut off,[14] and in marching they were like flowing water, and none of the soldiers of the three armies dared to transgress his prohibitions. So by basing himself on this one affair of Tien Hsieh, where a light offence was severely punished, Duke Wen caused the state of Chin to enjoy order.

Formerly Tan, Duke of Chou, killed his younger brother Kuan and banished his younger brother Huo, saying: 'They have transgressed against the interdicts.' The multitudes in the empire all said: 'If, when [the ruler's] own brothers commit a fault, he does not deviate from the law, how will it fare then with those who are distant and far off?' Therefore, the empire knew that sword and saw were applied to members of the court of Chou, and consequently all within the seas enjoyed order.[15] Therefore do I say: 'The climax in the understanding of punishments is to bring about a condition where there are no longer punishments.'

What I mean by the unification of education is that all those partisans of wide scholarship, sophistry, cleverness, good faith, integrity, rites and music, and moral culture, whether their reputations are unsullied or foul, should for these reasons not become rich or honoured, should not discuss punishments, and should not compose their private views independently and memorialise their superiors. The strong should be broken and the sharp be blunted.

Although one may be called a sage or wise or clever or eloquent or liberal or simple, yet one must not if one lacks merit, monopolise the ruler's favours, but the gate to riches and honour should lie in war and in nothing else. Those who are capable in war tread through the gate to riches and honour, but for the violent and self-willed there are inflexible punishments and no pardon. Thus

13 The expression 'to veer the fields towards the east' means that the farmers were ordered to plough their fields from east the west instead of from north to south, so that an army coming from Chin could easily follow the furrows and paths between the fields.

14 i.e. they could stop so suddenly.

15 The Duke of Chou, the famous brother of King Wu, had taken the regency at the latter's death (1116) and put an end to a conspiracy of his own brothers.

fathers and seniors, elder and younger brothers, acquaintances, relatives by marriage, husband and wife, one and all say that that, to which they devote special application, is war and that alone. Therefore indeed, the strong devote themselves to warfare, the old and feeble devote themselves to defence; for those who die there is no regret, and the living are bent on exerting themselves. This is what I mean by unifying education. The desire of people for riches and honour does not generally cease before their coffins are closed, and when the gate to riches and honour has its approach in soldiering, then when people hear of war, they congratulate each other, and whether at work or at rest, at times of drinking or eating, they will sing songs of war. This is what I mean by saying that the climax in the understanding of education is to bring about a condition where there is no longer education.

This is what I mean by the three teachings. A sage cannot have a universal knowledge of the needs of ten thousand beings; therefore in his administration of a state, he selects what is important for dealing with the ten thousand beings. So there is little instruction, but much successful effort. The way in which a sage governs a state is easy to know, but difficult to practise. Therefore, that sages need not be increased, commonplace rulers need not be abolished, that the killing of men is no violence and the rewarding of men no benevolence, follow from the fact that the law is clear. The sage confers office and grants rank according to merit, therefore men of talent are not anxious. The sage is not indulgent with transgressions and does not pardon crimes, and so villainy does not spring up. The sage, in administering a state, investigates the possibilities of uniformity, and that alone.

18 Policies

Of old, in the times of the Great and Illustrious Ruler,[1] people found their livelihood by cutting trees and slaying animals; the population was sparse, and trees and animals numerous. In the times of Huang-ti, neither young animals nor eggs were taken;[2] the officials had no provisions, and when the people died, they were not allowed to use outer coffins.[3] These measures were not the same, but that they both attained supremacy was due to the fact that the times in which they lived were different. In the times of Shen-nung, men ploughed to obtain food, and women wove to obtain clothing. Without the application of punishments or governmental measures, order prevailed; without the raising of mailed soldiers, he reigned supreme. After Shen-nung had died, the weak were conquered by force and the few oppressed by the many. Therefore Huang-ti created the ideas of prince and minister, of superior and inferior, the rites between father and son, between elder and younger brothers, the union between husband and wife, and between consort and mate. At home, he applied sword and saw, and abroad he used mailed soldiers; this was because the times had changed. Looking at it from this point of view, Shen-nung is not higher than Huang-ti, but the reason that his name was honoured was because he suited his time. Therefore, if by war one wishes to abolish war, even war is permissible; if by killing one wants to abolish killing, even killing is permissible; if by punishments one wishes to abolish punishments, even heavy punishments are permissible.

Of old, the one who could regulate the empire was he who regarded as his first task the regulating of his own people; the one

1 i.e. the mythical emperor Fu Hsi, usually called T'ai Hao.
2 Because the animals were so scarce.
3 Because of the lack of wood.

who could conquer a strong enemy was he who regarded as his first task the conquering of his own people. For the way in which the conquering of the people is based upon the regulating of the people is like the effect of smelting in regard to metal or the work of the potter in regard to clay; if the basis is not solid, then people are like flying birds or like animals. Who can regulate these? The basis of the people is the law. Therefore, a good ruler obstructed the people by means of the law, and so his reputation and his territory flourished. What is the cause of one's reputation becoming respected and one's territory wide, so that one attains sovereignty? [It is because one conquers in war.] What is the cause of one's reputation becoming debased and one's territory diminished, so that one comes to ruin? It is because one is worn out by war. From antiquity to the present time, it has never happened that one attained supremacy without conquest, or that one came to ruin without defeat. If the people are brave, one conquers in war, but if they are not brave, one is defeated in war. If one can unify the people for war, they are brave, but if one cannot unify the people for war, they are not brave. A sage-king obtains the kingship through the efforts of his soldiers. Therefore, he rouses the country and charges it with the obligation of military service. If one enters a state and sees its administration, it is strong if its people are of use. How does one know that the people are of use? If, on perceiving war, they behave like hungry wolves on seeing meat, then they are of use. Generally, war is a thing that people hate; he who succeeds in making people delight in war, attains supremacy. With the people of a strong state, the father in making a parting bequest to his son, the elder brother to his younger brother, the wife to her husband, all say: 'Do not return unless you win.' And further they say: 'If you incur death by failing in obedience to the law or by transgressing orders, we too shall die.' If in the villages they are governed in an orderly manner, then deserters from the ranks will have no resort and stragglers will have nowhere to go. By the order in the ranks they should be organised into bands of five; they should be distinguished by badges and controlled by mandates, so that there would be no place for bungling and no danger that exhaustion would arise. Thus the multitudes of the three armies obeyed the mandates like running water, and in danger of death they did not turn on their heels.

If a state is in disorder, it is not because the law is disorderly, but because its law is not applied. All states have laws, but there are no laws that guarantee that the laws are practised. All states have laws that prohibit crime and wickedness, and that punish thieves and robbers; but there are no laws that guarantee that criminals and wicked people, thieves and robbers, are caught. If those who commit crimes and wickedness, theft and robbery, are punished with death, and if, in spite of this, crime and wickedness, theft and robbery do not cease, then it is because they are not always caught. If they are always caught, and if, in spite of this, there still remain criminals, wicked people, thieves and robbers, then it is because punishments are too light. If punishments are light, one cannot exterminate them; but if they are always caught, then those who are punished will be numerous. Therefore, a good ruler punishes the bad people, but does not reward the virtuous ones; so without being punished, the people will be virtuous, and the reason of this is that punishments are heavy. When punishments are heavy, people dare not transgress, and therefore there will be no punishments; because none of the people will dare to do wrong, everyone in the whole country will be virtuous, so that without rewarding the virtuous, the people will be virtuous. That the rewarding of the virtuous is not permissible is because it is like giving rewards for not stealing. Therefore, a good ruler succeeds in making a man like Chih[4] trustworthy; how much more, then, a man like Po I![5] An incapable ruler makes a man like Po I mistrustful,; how much more a man like Chih! If conditions are such that one cannot commit crimes, then even a man like Chih will be trustworthy; but if conditions are such that it is possible to commit crimes, then even a man like Po I will be mistrustful.

A state either encourages orderly government, or it encourages disorder. If an intelligent ruler is on top, then those whom he appoints will be men of talent, and thus the law will be adhered to by the people of talent. If the law is adhered to by people of talent, then there will be law amongst those below, and the worthless will

4 A notorious robber of the time of Confucius, who was said to have been the younger brother of the virtuous Liu-hsia Hui; cf. Mencius iiib, 10 (3).
5 12th century BC. A man of lofty character; cf. Mencius iia, 2 (22) et al.

not dare to commit crimes. This is what I call 'encouraging orderly government'. But if an unintelligent ruler is on top, then those whom he appoints will certainly be worthless men, so that there will be no clear law in the state and worthless people will dare to commit crimes. This is what I call 'encouraging disorder'. An army either encourages strength or it encourages weakness. If the people desire naturally to fight and are not left without fighting, it is called 'encouraging strength', but if the people naturally do not desire to fight and are left without fighting, it is called 'encouraging weakness'.

An intelligent ruler does not enrich and honour his ministers in an arbitrary manner. What I mean by riches are not grain, rice, pearls or jade, and what I mean by honour are not rank, position, office or appointments; but I mean the riches and honour of rank and emoluments acquired by actions contrary to the law and which are prompted by selfish interest.[6] Generally a ruler of men does not, in virtuous conduct, exceed other men, nor does he do so in knowledge, nor does he surpass others in courage or strength, yet the people, though they may have sages and wise men, they dare not plot against him; though they may have courage, dare not kill him; though they are numerous, they dare not over-rule their lord; though the people may reach a number of many tens of thousands, if heavy rewards are set before them, they dare not contest for them; if penalties are applied, they dare not resent them. The reason is that there is law. If a state is in disorder, it is because the people often have private opinions of what is their duty; if an army is weak, it is because people often have private shows of bravery, and as a result there will be dismemberment. If the roads to the acquirement of titles and emoluments are many, ruin will ensue. In a country where the desire is to cheapen rank and to make light of emoluments, officials draw their salaries without activity, men have fame without acquiring it in war, people have respect without having the rank that entitles them to it, are rich without having

6 The meaning, which is explained in what follows, is that the ruler does not withhold the customary rewards and distinctions for public services, but that he should not use his servants for illegal and selfish purposes and reward them specially for actions of that nature.

emoluments, and are leaders without having office; such are said to be a wicked people.

He who is called a virtuous ruler has no loyal ministers, and a compassionate father has no filial sons. If it is desired to do away with clever talkers, then all should control one another by means of the law, and should correct one another by means of mandates. Being unable to do wrong alone, one will not do wrong in the company of others. What is called wealth is to have receipts large and expenditure small. When there is moderation in dress and frugality in food and drink, then expenditure is small. When women within and men outside fulfil their duties completely, then receipts are large. What is called intelligence is for nothing to escape the sight, so that the multitude of officials dare not commit crimes, nor the people dare to do wrong. Thus the ruler of men will repose on a rest-couch and listen to the sound of stringed and bamboo instruments, and yet the empire will enjoy order. In other words, what is called intelligence is to cause the masses to have no possibility of not working. What is called strength is to conquer the empire; by conquering the empire, all the forces are united, and as a result the brave and strong will not dare to commit any violence, nor will sages and wise men dare to deceive or to be employed on empty grounds. When the multitudes of the empire are united, none will dare not to do what he [the ruler] likes, but all will avoid what he dislikes. In other words, what is called strength is to cause all bravery and force to have no possibility of being used except for the prince's own advantage. If the prince's will is effective, the empire will benefit by it; if it is ineffective, the empire will blame him.

Whoever relies on the empire is rejected by the empire; whoever relies on himself, gains the empire. The one who gains the empire is he who regards it as his first duty to gain himself; the one who succeeds in conquering a strong enemy is he who regards it as his first duty to conquer himself.

A sage knows the right principles which must be followed, and the right time and circumstances for action. Therefore the rule which he exercises always leads to order, the people whom he employs in war are always brave, and the commands which he issues are always obeyed. In consequence, when his army marches out, it has no equal, and when his commands are issued, the whole empire submits.

A yellow crane flies a thousand *li* at one stretch, because it is supplied with those qualities which make it fit for flying. The Ch'i-lin and the Lü-êrh cover a thousand *li* a day, because they are supplied with the power needed for running. Tigers, leopards, bears and yellow bears are unmatched in fierce fighting, because they have the nature fitted for conquest. A sage views the fundamental elements of government, and knows the principle which must be followed; therefore, his way of directing the people is like directing water from a high to a low place, or like directing fire towards dry things and away from wet ones. Therefore is it said: 'The benevolent may be benevolent towards others, but cannot cause others to be benevolent; the righteous may love others, but cannot cause others to love.' From this I know that benevolence and righteousness are not sufficient for governing the empire. A sage has a nature that insists on good-faith, and he also has a law [method] by which he compels the whole empire to have good faith. What is called righteousness is when ministers are loyal, sons filial, when there are proper ceremonies between juniors and seniors, and distinctions between men and women, when a hungry man eats, and a dying man lives, not improperly, but only in accordance with righteousness This, however, is the constant condition when there is law. A sage-king does not value righteousness, but he values the law. If with the law one sees to it that it is clear, and with commands that they are carried out, then it will be all right.

CHAPTER 5

19 Within the Borders

Within the four frontiers, men and women are known by name to their superiors; at birth they are registered and at death they are erased. Those who have rank ask of those who have no rank to act as bodyguard; for each degree the service of one man is requested. When they have no military service, the bodyguards serve their great officers six days in the month; in times of military service, they follow their great officers and are fed by them. The military ranks from the first degree down to the small prefects are called *hsiao, t'u, ts'ao, shih*; the public ranks from the second degree upwards to the degree of *pu-keng* are called military officials, *tsu*. In battle five men are organised into a squad; if one of them is killed, the other four are beheaded. If a man can capture one head then he is exempted from taxes.

For every five men is there a corporal, *t'un-chang*, and for every hundred men a centurion, *chiang*. If in a battle the centurions and corporals are unsuccessful, they are beheaded; if they are successful, thirty-three heads or more are accounted ample, and to the centurions and corporals one degree in rank is given. An officer of 500 men has 50 swordsmen with short weapons;[1] an officer of twice 500 men, in commanding them has 100 swordsmen; a prefect with an income of 1,000 *piculs* of grain has 100 swordsmen; a prefect with an income of 800 *piculs* of grain has 80 swordsmen; one with 700 *piculs* has 70 swordsmen; one with 600 *piculs* has 60 swordsmen; the *kuo-wei* has 1,000 swordsmen, and the general has 4,000 swordsmen. If in a battle, it comes so far that he is killed, then the swordsmen are beheaded. If a man can capture one head, he is exempted from taxes. If in attacking a city or besieging a town they

1 'Short weapons', such as swords, as distinguished from bows, used at long distance.

can capture 8,000 heads or more, it is accounted ample; if in a battle in the open field they take 2,000 heads, it is accounted ample. From the *ts'ao* officers up to *hsiao* officers, the great general fully rewards the officers in the ranks. He who was formerly *kung-shih* is promoted to *shang-tsao*; a *shang-tsao* to *tsan-niao*; a *tsan-niao* to *pu-keng*; a *pu-keng* to great officer, *ta-fu*.

When an officer is raised to the rank of a district commander, *hsien-wei*,[2] then he is presented with six prisoner slaves, and provided with 5,000 soldiers and an income of 600 *piculs* of grain; *ta-fu* are raised to the rank of *kuo-wei*; one who was formerly a *ta-fu* is promoted to *kung-ta-fu*; a *kung-ta-fu* to *kung-sheng*; a *kung-sheng* to *wu-ta-fu*, and then receives a taxpaying city of 300 families. A former *wu-ta-fu* is promoted to *shu-chang*: a *shu-chang* to a *tso-keng*; one of the three *kengs* to a *ta-liang-tsao*. In all these cases there is presented a town of 300 families, or the taxes of 300. Where there is a taxpaying town of 600 families, an office of vice-chancellor is conferred. Those who ride in the company of the great general are all promoted three degrees. He who was formerly assistant chancellor, when he is accounted to have the full merit, is promoted to the actual chancellorship.

When three heads are captured in battle, they are exposed for three days; the general confers, in the cases where there is no doubt that it is deserved, the titles of *shih* and *ta-fu* in reward. When the heads have been hanging for three days and no titles of *shih* or *ta-fu* have been conferred on any one in reward, then they are removed. The four *wei* of a district are under the critical supervision of a. *ch'eng-wei*. If he succeeds in capturing the head of a man of rank, he receives one *ch'ing*[3] of land and nine *mu* of estate, apart from the conferment of one degree of rank and a bodyguard for each rank, and he is allowed to enter amongst the military officers. In case of transgression of the law, then those of higher rank criticise those of lower rank and degree. If a man of high rank has been cashiered, he may not be given as servant to a man of rank. Those holding rank from the second degree upwards, in case of an offence, are degraded; those holding rank not higher than

2 Under the Ch'in dynasty, in each district there were two military commanders.

3 One *ch'ing* is 100 *mu*.

the first degree, when guilty of an offence, lose it. At the death of a *hsiao-fu* up to a *ta-fu*, coffins should be of a different kind for each degree, and the number of trees on the graves should be one for each degree in rank. In attacking a city or besieging a town, the minister of public works of the state examines critically the size and resources of that city. The *kuo-wei* assigns the places, dividing the area according to the number of *t'u* and *hsiao* officers for the attack, and he sets them a time-limit, saying: 'Those who are first will be rewarded as the vanguard and those who hold back will be reprimanded, as being in the rear, and on a second reprimand will be dismissed.' They dig out subterranean passages and pile up fuel; when the fuel has been piled up they set fire to the beams. From the corps of sappers, on each side of the town, there are eighteen men. The soldiers from the corps of sappers, if they know how to fight fiercely, although they cannot capture the heads of any men in the ranks, are rewarded with one degree for each man; for every one man that is killed, freedom from taxes is given, and for every one man that cannot fight to the death, ten are torn to pieces by chariots.[4] Those who make critical remarks are branded or their noses are sliced off under the city wall. The *kuo-wei*, in assigning their various places to all, cause the several detachments to be followed by *chung-tsu*. The general erects a wooden platform, from which, together with the chief supervisor of the state and the chief secretary, he watches [the battle]. Those who enter first are rewarded as men of the vanguard, and those who enter last are treated as men of the rearguard; as to the corps of sappers, the utmost use is made of their few men; if these few men are not sufficient, they are supplemented by those who are anxious to receive a rank.

---

4 The idea of this uncertain paragraph seems to be that the responsibility of the corps of sappers is especially great. If they show bravery, although they capture no heads, yet by special favour they receive the same rewards as those who do capture heads; but on the other hand, in case of cowardice, they are held mutually responsible and ten men are punished for one man's fault.

20 *Weakening the People*

A weak people means a strong state and a strong state means a weak people. Therefore, a country which has the right way is concerned with weakening the people. If they are simple they become strong, and if they are licentious they become weak. Being weak, they are law-abiding; being licentious, they let their ambition go too far; being weak, they are serviceable; but if they let their ambition go too far, they will become strong.[1] Therefore is it said: 'To remove the strong by means of a strong people brings weakness; to remove the strong by means of a weak people brings strength.' The people, if they are benefited, are harmonious, and if they are loved, they are serviceable; being serviceable, they receive appointments, and being harmonious, they are not deficient. Receiving appointments, they will enrich themselves in government positions, the ruler will abandon the law and allow things to be done for the benefit of the people. Thus criminals will be numerous. If the people are poor, they will be rich in strength, and being rich in strength, they become licentious; being licentious, they will suffer from the parasites. Therefore, if the people are rich and unemployed, they should be made to obtain titles by means of their grain, and every one of them will certainly become strong. Then there will be no derogation of agriculture, and the six parasites will not sprout out, and thus, the state being rich and the people orderly, there will be twofold strength.

An army easily becomes weak, but it is difficult to keep it strong. The people enjoy life and feel happy in leisure, but find it difficult to risk death in dangers. If they find it easy, they will be strong. If there are things that one is ashamed of doing, in the case where there are many crimes and few rewards, there is no loss; and in the case where there are many crimes and the suspicion falls on the

1 The meaning seems to be that whereas, on the one hand, licence weakens the people, on the other hand, it gives them also the chance of developing the six 'parasites'.

enemy, the loss will certainly become gain and the army will become extremely strong and redoubtable. If there are no things which one is ashamed of doing, it is of advantage to use the army, and if one retains the advantage for a long time, one's position will become assuredly supreme. Therefore, if one's army accomplishes what the enemy dares not accomplish, one becomes strong, and if affairs are undertaken which the enemy is ashamed to perform, one obtains advantage.

If there is law and the people are quiet, changes made by the ruler are relegated to the second place, so that affairs become well organised; the country is interested in maintaining peace and quiet, but a ruler in wielding his authority and privileged position; thus a ruler values many changes, but the country values few changes.

If the profit leaks out through only one outlet, the state will have many products, but if it leaks out through ten outlets, the state will have few products. If only one outlet is preserved, there will be orderly government; but if ten outlets are preserved, there will be disorder. Orderly government brings strength, but disorder brings weakness; when there is strength, products are imported, but when there is weakness, products are exported. Therefore a state that imports products is strong and one that exports products is weak.

If the people live in humiliation, they value rank; if they are weak, they honour office; and if they are poor, they prize rewards. If the people are governed by means of punishments, they enjoy service, and if the people are made to fight by means of rewards, they scorn death. Therefore if, in war, one's army is efficient, one is called strong. If the people have private honours, they hold rank cheap and disdain office; if they are rich, they think lightly of rewards. Orderly people are ashamed of humiliations, and if they are made to fight by means of punishments, they will fight; if in fighting people are afraid of death and behave in a disorderly manner, the result will be that soldiers and farmers will be lazy and the country weak.

Farming, trade and office are the three permanent functions in a state. Farmers open up the soil, merchants import products, officials rule the people. These three functions give rise to parasites, six in number, which are called: care for old age, living on others, beauty, love, ambition and virtuous conduct. If these six parasites find an attachment, there will be dismemberment. If farmers live in affluence, they seek leisure in their old age; if merchants have illicit profits, there will be beauty and love, and these will harm the means for enforcing the law; if officials are set up, but are not utilised, ambition and virtuous conduct will be the end. If the six parasites become a pervading custom, the army will certainly suffer great defeats.

If the law is crooked, order turns into disorder; if reliance is placed on virtue, there is much talking; if government measures are numerous, the state is in disorder; and if there is much talking, the army is weak. But if the law is clear, government measures are limited; if reliance is placed on force, talking ceases; if government measures are limited, the country enjoys orderly administration; and if talking ceases, the army is strong.

Therefore, in ruling a great country it becomes small, and in ruling a small country it becomes great. If the government takes such measures as the people hate, the people are made weak; and if it takes such measures as the people like, the people are made strong. But a weak people means a strong state, and a strong people means a weak state. If the government takes such measures as the people like, they are made strong, and if strong people are made even stronger, the army becomes doubly weak; but if the government takes such measures as the people hate, they are made weak, and if weak people are made even weaker, the army becomes doubly strong. Therefore, by strengthening the people one becomes doubly weak and perishes; by weakening the people one becomes doubly strong and attains supremacy. With a strong people to attack, the strong brings weakness, whereas on the other side strength remains; with a weak people to attack, the strong brings strength, whereas on the other side strength is removed. If strength remains on the other side, one perishes, but if strength is removed on the other side, one attains supremacy. Therefore, with a strong people to attack, the strong brings dismemberment, but with a weak people to attack, the strong brings supremacy.

The way in which an intelligent ruler uses his ministers is by always giving them employment for merits which they have acquired, and by always fully recognising their exertions by rewards; and if a ruler of men makes his people believe in this as firmly as they do in the sun and moon, then he will have no equal.

Now Li Lou could see the tip of an autumn's hair, but he could not transfer his sharp vision to others; Wu Huo could lift the weight of 1,000 *chün*, but he could not transfer his great strength to others. So sages and men of talent are bound to their personality and nature, which cannot be transferred to others.

Now, those who administer affairs in our times all desire to be more than sages; there is much talk of setting the law on high, but they rule in defiance of the law. This is like carrying a heavy load along a far road without having a horse or an ox, or like crossing a wide river without having a boat or oars.

Now, to have a numerous population and a strong army is the great capital of an emperor or king, but if he does not have clear laws by which to keep them, he is next door to peril and ruin. Therefore an intelligent ruler studies the law, and thus understands how to bring it about that the people within his borders have no perverse and depraved hearts, that idly-living scholars are pressed into the battle line, and that the ten thousand subjects are alert in ploughing and warfare.

The people of the state of Ch'u, who were alert and well-balanced and fast as a whirlwind, were, with their iron lances made of the steel from Yüan, as sharp as a bee's sting. As armour they wore the skin of sharks and the hide of rhinoceros, which are as strong as metal and stone. The Yang-tzŭ and the Han Rivers were its moats, and the Ju and the Ying[2] its boundaries; the Forest of Teng[3] was its screen, and the Wall of the Fang Mountains[4] was its frontier. Yet when the army of Ch'in marched on Yen and Ying,[5] it took those cities as easily as if it had been merely the shaking of a dead tree. T'ang Mieh[6] met his death at Ch'ui-shê,[7] Chuang

2 Rivers in Honan which after joining become a tributary of the Huai.

3 South of the present prefecture of Hsiang-yang in Hu-pei.

4 The Fang Mountains were in the north-east of Hu-pei; there was a wall of some 10 *li*.

5 In 279 BC the King of Ch'in took Yen, and in 278, Ying. Yen was south of the sub-prefecture I-ch'eng,, in the prefecture of Hsiang-yang in Hu-pei; Ying was the capital of Ch'u, situated 10 *li* north of Chiang-ling, in the prefecture of Ching-chou in Hu-pei.

6 The general of Ch'u.

7 Hsün-tzŭ reads Ch'ui-sha; its locality is unknown. The battle occurred in 301 BC. In the Annals of Ch'in, Ssu-ma Ch'ien reports this battle in 299 BC.

Ch'iao[8] rose in the interior, and Ch'u was divided into five parts.

This was not because its territory was not large or that the population was not numerous, or that the armour and weapons and resources were not many, but the reason that in fighting it did not win and in defending it was unable to hold its own, was due to the fact that it did not have law.

He who dismisses scales and standard weights and manipulates light and heavy . . . [9]

---

8 Chang Ch'iao had been ordered by King Wei of Ch'u (339-329 BC) to pacify the central part of Yun-nan and had there created a principality for himself.

9 This is a fragment which does not seem to belong here.

21

(Lost)

22 External and Internal Affairs

Of the external affairs of the people, there is nothing more difficult than warfare, so an easy law cannot bring them to it. What is called an easy law? It is when rewards are few and authority weak, and when depraved doctrines are not obstructed. What are called depraved doctrines? They are when sophistry and knowledge are valued, when itinerant politicians receive office, and when scholarship and private reputations are in evidence. When these three are not barred, then people will not fight and affairs fail. For when rewards are few, then there is no advantage in obedience; when authority is weak, then there is no harm in transgression. Therefore depraved doctrines are started in order to mislead the people; and to make them fight while the law is easy is like setting a cat to bait a rat. Is that not impossible? Therefore, he who desires to make his people fight sees to it that the law is severe; consequently rewards will be numerous, authority will be strict, depraved doctrines will be obstructed, those engaged in sophistry and knowledge will not be honoured, itinerant politicians will not be employed in office, scholarship and private reputations will not be in evidence. If rewards are numerous and authority strict, then people, seeing that in war rewards are many, will forget the danger of death, and seeing their degradation when there is no war, will find life hard. When rewards make them forget the danger of death, and strict authority causes them to find life hard, and moreover depraved doctrines are barred, in this manner meeting the enemy would be like shooting, with a crossbow of a hundred *piculs'* capacity, a floating leaf. How would it be possible for it not to perish?

Of the internal affairs of the people, there is nothing harder than agriculture. Therefore an easy administration cannot bring them to it. What is called an easy administration? When farmers are poor and merchants are rich, when clever people gain profit and itinerant office-seekers are numerous. So the farmers, in spite of their extremely hard labour, gain little profit, and are worse off than merchants and shopkeepers and all manner of clever people. If one succeeds in restricting the number of these latter, then even if one wished to, one could not prevent a state from becoming rich. Therefore is it said: 'If one wishes to enrich the country through agriculture, then within the borders grain must be dear, taxes for those who are not farmers must be many, and dues on market-profit must be heavy, with the result that people are forced to have land. As those who have no land are obliged to buy their grain, grain will be dear, and those who have land will thus profit. When those who have land gain profit, there will be many who will occupy themselves [with agriculture].' When grain is dear, and the dealing in it is not profitable, while, moreover, heavy taxes are imposed, then people cannot fail to abolish merchants and shop-keepers and all manner of clever folk, and to occupy themselves in the profit from the soil. So the strength of the people will be fully exerted in the profit from the soil. Therefore, he who organises a state should let his soldiers have the full benefit of the profits on the frontiers, and let the farmers have the full benefit from the profits of the market. If the first happens, the state will be strong, and if the second happens, it will be rich. Therefore one who abroad is strong in warfare, and at home is rich in peace, attains supremacy. For if grain is cheap, the value of money is high, and cheap grain means poor farmers, and a high value of money means rich merchants; and if secondary occupations are not forbidden, then . . .

23 Prince and Minister

In the days of antiquity, before the time when there were princes and ministers, superiors and inferiors, the people were disorderly and were not well administered, and so the sages made a division between the noble and the humble; they regulated rank and position, and established names and appellations, in order to distinguish the ideas of prince and minister, of superior and inferior. As the territory was extensive, the people numerous and all things many, they made a division of five kinds of officials, and maintained it; as the people were numerous, wickedness and depravity originated, so in order to prohibit them, they established laws and regulations and created weights and measures, and in consequence there were the idea of prince and minister, the distinctions between the five kinds of officials, and the interdicts of the laws and regulations, to which it was necessary to pay heed. If, when occupying the position of prince, one's mandates are not carried out, one is in peril; when there is no constancy in the distinctions between the five kinds of officials, there is disorder; when laws and regulations have been set up and yet private notions of virtue are practised, then people do not stand in fear of punishment. When the prince is respected, his mandates are carried out; when officials have been well-trained, there is constancy; and when laws and regulations are clear, people stand in fear of punishment. If laws and regulations are not clear, then it is impossible to obtain from the people the observance of mandates. If the people do not observe the mandates, but you want the prince to be respected, even a man with the wisdom of Yao and Shun would not be able to govern well. The way in which an intelligent prince administers the empire is to do so according to the law, and to reward according to merit. It is the hankering for rank and emoluments that prompts people to fight energetically and not to shun death. The way in which an intelligent prince administers a state is to reward soldiers who have had the merit of making decapitations or capturing prisoners, with such rank as will really give honour, and to grant them such emoluments as will be sufficient for them to live on – and to farmers who do not leave their ground, sufficient to nourish both their parents and to keep their family affairs in order. Thus soldiers in the army will fulfil their duty even to death, and farmers will not be negligent.

But the princes of the present time do not act thus. They relax the law and keep to knowledge; they turn their backs on merit and keep to people of reputation. Therefore, soldiers do not fight and farmers are migratory.

I have heard that the gate through which the people are guided depends on where their superiors lead. Therefore, whether one succeeds in making people farm or fight, or in making them into travelling politicians, or in making them into scholars, depends on what their superiors encourage. If their superiors encourage merit and labour, people will fight; if they encourage the Odes and Book of History, people will become scholars. For people's attitude towards profit is just like the tendency of water to flow downwards, without preference for any of the four sides. The people are only interested in obtaining profit, and it depends on what their superiors encourage, what they will do. If men with angry eyes, who clench their fists and call themselves brave, are successful; if men in flowing robes, who idly talk, are successful; if men who waste their time and spend their days in idleness, and save their efforts for obtaining benefit through private channels, are successful – if these three kinds of people, though they have no merit, all obtain respectful treatment, then people will leave off farming and fighting and will do this: either they will extort it by discussions and suggestions, or they will ask for it by practising flattery, or they will struggle for it by acts of bravery. Thus farmers and fighters will dwindle daily, and itinerant office-seekers will increase more and more, with the result that the country will fall into disorder, the land will be dismembered, the army will be weak and the ruler debased. This would be the result of relaxing laws and regulations and placing reliance on men of fame and reputation. Therefore is an intelligent ruler cautious with regard to laws and regulations; he does not hearken to words which are not in accordance with the law; he does not exalt actions which are not in accordance with the law; he does not perform deeds which are not in accordance with the law. But he hearkens to words which are in accordance with the law; he exalts actions which are in accordance with the law; he performs deeds which are in accordance with the law. Thus the state will enjoy order, the land will be wide, the army will be strong, and the ruler will be honoured. This is the climax of good government, and it is imperative for a ruler of men to examine it.

24 Interdicts and Encouragements

The method by which a ruler of men prohibits and encourages is by means of rewards and penalties. Rewards follow merit and penalties follow crime; therefore is it necessary to be careful in appraising merit and in investigating crime. Now, rewards exalt and punishments debase, but if the superiors have no definite knowledge of their method, it is no better than if they had no method at all. But the method for right knowledge is power and figures. Therefore, the early kings did not rely on their strength but on their power (*shih*); they did not rely on their belief but on their figures. Now, for example, a floating seed of the *p'eng* plant, meeting a whirlwind, may be carried a thousand *li*, because it rides on the power (*shih*) of the wind. If, in measuring an abyss, you know that it is a thousand fathoms deep, it is owing to the figures which you find by dropping a string. So by depending on the power (*shih*) of a thing, you will reach a point, however distant it may be; and by keeping the proper figures, you will find out the depth, however deep it may be. Now, for example, in the darkness of the night even a Li Lou cannot see a great mountain forest, but in the clear morning light, with the brilliant sun, he can distinguish the flying birds above, and below he can see an autumn hair; for the vision of the eye is dependent on the power of the sun. When the highest condition of power (*shih*) is reached, things are arranged without a multitude of officials and are made fitting by expounding the system. But nowadays reliance is placed on a multitude of offices and a host of civil servants, and in the official bureaux assistants and controllers are appointed. Now, the idea of appointing these assistants and controllers is indeed to prevent men from making profit, but these assistants and controllers themselves also desire to make profit. How then can they prevent others from doing so! Therefore, if one relies on assistants and controllers for one's administration, then will it be an administration that can barely maintain itself.

It is not thus, if one understands 'system'; one separates their power (*shih*) and puts checks on their conduct. Therefore is it said: 'If the conditions of power (*shih*) are such that it is difficult to conceal anything, then even a man like Chih does no wrong.' Therefore, the early kings prized power (*shih*). Some say: 'A ruler of men holds a nominal right of consent, *post factum*; then things are controlled and examined, and by this control wickedness is discovered.' I do not think that this is right. For officials exert sole authority and take decisions a thousand *li* away [from the ruler]. In the twelfth month, to confirm it, they make a report, in which the affairs of the whole year have separate entries; but as the ruler gives but one hearing, although he sees doubtful cases, he cannot determine whether an official is capable or otherwise. . . . [1]

For example, if objects come near, the eye cannot but see them; if words are insistent, the ear cannot but hear them; for if objects approach, they alter in appearance, and if words draw near, they form coherent speech. So with the organisation in a well-governed state: people cannot escape punishment any more than the eyes can hide from the mind what they see. But in the disorderly states of the present time, it is not thus: reliance is placed on a multitude of offices and a host of civil servants, but however numerous the civil servants may be, their affairs are the same and they belong to one body. Now, those whose affairs are the same and who belong to one body, cannot control one another. But by making their interests different and their disadvantages dissimilar, the early kings created guarantees. Therefore, in a condition of complete good government, husband and wife and friends cannot abandon each other's evil, cover up wrongdoing and not cause harm to relatives; nor can the men from the people mutually conceal each other from their superiors and government servants. That is because, although their affairs are connected, their interests are different. But now-adays a Tsou and a Yü cannot control each other, because their business is the same and their interests are also similar . . . Suppose that horses could speak, then a Tsou and a Yü would have no chance of escaping what they find hateful; that is because their interests would be

---

1 There is probably a gap in the text here.

different.[2] When interests are connected and what they hate is the same, then a father cannot reprimand his son, nor a prince his minister. The relation of government servants to other government servants is this, that their interests are connected and what they hate is the same. Now, the early kings made it a principle that those whose business was connected, should have different interests. Though the people may hide things from their ruler, there is no harm done in thus covering up, nor can there be advantage in having virtuous men or harm in having worthless ones. The system, therefore, of good government is to neglect the virtuous and to abolish the wise.

2 i.e. the interests of the horses and of these officials are different, so that the horses, could they but speak, would denounce their faults.

25 Attention to Law

Generally, there is no one in the world who does not base order on the causes of disorder. Therefore, to a limited degree of order corresponds a limited degree of disorder, and to a great degree of order corresponds a great degree of disorder. There is no ruler of men who can give order to his people for all time, nor is there a country in the world that has not known disorder. What do I mean by saying that one bases order on the causes of disorder? Raising virtuous and capable men is the cause of bringing order into the world, but it is also the cause of order becoming disorder. Those whom the world calls virtuous are men whose words are upright. The reason why they are regarded as upright in words is due to their partisans. Hearing their words, one takes them to be capable, and on asking their partisans, one thinks that they are indeed so. Therefore, one prizes them without waiting for them to acquire actual merit, or one punishes them without waiting for them to commit crimes. In these circumstances, vile officials are given precisely the opportunity to accomplish their wicked and danger-ous acts, and small-minded men have an opportunity to apply their dexterous and crafty tricks.[1] If in the beginning a basis for wicked-ness and craftiness is provided for officials and people, then if finally one tries to make them correct and guileless, even [a great sage like] Yü could not succeed in causing as many as ten men to be like that. How then could an ordinary ruler manage the people of the whole country in this way?

Those people who form parties with others do not need Us[2] for obtaining success, and if superiors pull one way with the people, then the latter will turn their backs on the ruler's position and will turn towards private connections. When this is the case, the prince will be weak and his ministers strong, and if the ruler does

1 The idea is that if people are to be promoted on account of the reputations they have, there would be much room for the arbitrary acts of bad officials.
2 A figure of speech, meaning the ruler.

not understand this, then if the country is not annexed by the feudal lords, it will be robbed by the people.

Both stupid and wise will alike try to acquire that power of eloquence, and if scholars study with those eloquent speakers, then people will lose touch with reality and will recite empty phrases. Should this be the case, then their strength will decrease and wrongdoing will increase; and if the prince does not understand it, in battle he will lose his generals, and in defence his cities will certainly be sold. Therefore, if there is an intelligent ruler or a loyal minister born in this age who wishes to lead his country, then he should not for one moment be forgetful of the law, but he should conquer and destroy cabals, control and abolish eloquence; and relying on the law, the country will enjoy order. If a condition is brought about where, for government servants, there is no other standard maintained than the law, then however tricky they may be, they will be unable to commit wickedness; and if, for the people, a condition is brought about where there is no other way of exerting their capacities than in war, then however great the danger may be, no deceit will be possible. Indeed, if people control each other by law and recommend each other by following systematic rules, then they cannot benefit each other with praise nor harm each other with slander. If the people see that there is no benefit in praising each other, they will become used to loving each other without flattery, and if they see that there is no harm in slandering each other, they will become used to hating each other without injuring each other. If the love of men does not mean flattery, and the hatred of men does not mean causing injury, then both love and hatred will be pure, which is the highest degree of order. Therefore do I say: 'If one relies on law, the country will enjoy order.'

A country of a thousand chariots is able to preserve itself by defence, and a country of ten thousand chariots is able to round itself off by fighting – even [a bad ruler like] Chieh would not be able to twist one word of this statement in order to subdue his enemies;[3] and if abroad one is incapable of waging war, and at home one is incapable of defence, then even [a good ruler like] Yao could not pacify, for any misbehaviour, a country that [normally]

---

3 i.e. subdue his enemies by any other means than fighting.

would be no match. Looking at it from this point of view, that through which the country is important and that through which the ruler is honoured is force. Force being the basis of both, how is it then that no ruler on earth succeeds in developing force? Bring about a condition where people find it bitter not to till, and where they find it dangerous not to fight. These are two things which filial sons, though they dislike them, do for their fathers' sake, and loyal ministers, though they dislike them, do for their sovereign's sake. Nowadays, if you wish to stimulate the multitude of people to make them do what even filial sons and loyal ministers dislike doing, I think it is useless unless you compel them by means of punishments, and stimulate them by means of rewards. But nowadays, the ordinary types of ruler all neglect laws and measures, and rely on sophistry and cleverness; they push back men of merit and force, and advance those of benevolence and righteousness, with the result that people do not devote themselves to agriculture and warfare. If such people do not turn their energies to agriculture, at home their food-supply will be exhausted; and if they do not turn to their duty in warfare, abroad the army will be weak; then, though one may have a territory of ten thousand *li*, and a million armed men, it will be the same as a plain that has to depend on its own resources. Furthermore, the early kings were able to command their people to walk on bare swords and to suffer arrows and stones, and the people were willing to do so, not because they liked learning such things, but because they escaped harm[4] thereby. Therefore my teaching is to issue such orders that people, if they are desirous of profit, can attain their aim only by agriculture, and if they want to avoid harm, can only escape it by war. There will be no one within the borders who will not devote himself at first to ploughing and fighting, in order thereby later to obtain that which gives him pleasure. Therefore, though the territory may be small, the produce will be plentiful, and though the population may be sparse, the army will be strong. If one can achieve these two things within the territory, then the road to becoming a lord-protector or king of the whole empire is fully prepared.

4 i.e. punishment.

26 The Fixing of Rights and Duties

The Duke questioned Kung-sun Yang, saying: 'Supposing that one established laws and mandates today, and wished that tomorrow all government servants and people throughout the empire should understand them clearly and apply them, so that all should be as one, and should have no selfish intentions – how can one bring this about?'

Kung-sun Yang replied: 'There should be instituted, for the laws, government officers who are able to understand the contents of the decrees, and who should be the regulators of the empire. Then they should memorialise the Son of Heaven, whereupon the Son of Heaven would personally preside over the law and promulgate it. All should then issue to their inferiors the mandates they have received, and the law officers should preside personally over the law and promulgate it. When people venture to neglect practising the items[1] named in the promulgations of the officers presiding over the law, then each one is punished according to the item in the law which he has neglected. In the eventuality of these officers who preside over the law being transferred or dying, students should be made to read the contents of the law, and a standard of knowledge should be fixed for them, so that within a certain number of days they should know the contents of the law; and for those students who do not reach the standard, a law is made for punishing them. Should any one dare to tamper with the text of the law, to erase or add one single character, or more, he shall be condemned to death without pardon. Whenever government officials or people have questions to ask of the officers presiding over the law about the meaning of the laws or mandates, the officers should in each case answer clearly according to the laws and mandates about which it was originally desired to ask questions; and they should in each case prepare a tablet of the length of 1 foot 6 inches, on which should be

1 'names', i.e. the headings or items of the law.

distinctly inscribed the year, month, day and hour, as well as the items of law about which questions were asked, for the information of the government officials or of the people. Should the officers who preside over the law not give the desired information, they should be punished according to the contents of the law; that is, they should be punished according to the law about which the government officials or people have asked information. The officers presiding over the law should forthwith give to those government officials who ask information about the law, the left half of the document, and they themselves should store carefully the wooden bindings with the right half of the document, keep them in a room, and seal them with the seal of the chief of the office of laws and mandates. Later, on the death of the officer, affairs should be transacted according to these files. All the laws and mandates should be put together as a set, one set being kept in the palace of the Son of Heaven. Forbidden archives should be built for the laws, which are locked with lock and key to prevent admittance, and are sealed up; herein should be stored one set of the laws and mandates. Inside the forbidden archives they should be sealed with a seal forbidding their opening. Whoever ventures unauthorisedly to break the seals of the forbidden archives, or to enter the forbidden archives, to inspect the forbidden laws and mandates, or to tamper with one or more characters of the forbidden laws, shall, in any of these cases, be guilty of death without pardon. Once a year laws and mandates shall be received for prohibitions and orders to be issued. The Son of Heaven shall set up three law officers, one in the palace, one in the office of the *Yü-shih*,[2] together with a government official, and one in the chancery of the *Ch'eng-hsiang*.[3] In the various prefectures and sub-prefectures of the feudal lords shall be instituted one law officer, together with government officials, all of whom shall be similar to the law officers in Ch'in. Thus the prefectures and sub-prefectures and the feudal lords shall all alike receive a knowledge of the laws and mandates in the archives, and moreover the afore-mentioned government officials and people, who are desirous of

2 The *Yu-shih-ta-fu* under the Ch'in dynasty was in charge of all the plans and official documents. He was the third in rank.
3 The *Ch'eng-hsiang* was the Grand Councillor, the highest office.

knowing the law, shall all address their inquiries to these law officers. Thus there shall be no one among the government officials and people of the empire who does not know the law, and as the officials are clearly aware that the people know the laws and mandates, they dare not treat the people contrary to the law, nor dare the people transgress the law, as they would come into conflict with the law officers. If in their treatment of the people the government officials do not act according to the law, the former should inquire of the law officer, who should at once inform them of the punishment [for the illegal action in question] fixed by the law. The people should then at once inform the government officials, formally, of the law officer's statement. Thus the government officials, knowing that such is the course of events, dare not treat the people contrary to the law, nor do the people dare infringe the law. In this way, government officials and the people of the empire, however virtuous or good, however sophistical or sagacious they may be, cannot add one word to twist the law; nor, though they may have a thousand pieces of gold, can they use one twenty-fourth of an ounce of it for such a purpose. Thus the knowing and crafty ones, as well as the virtuous and capable, will all force themselves to behave well and will do their best to restrain themselves and to serve the public weal. When people are stupid, they are easy to govern. All this originates from the fact that the law is clear, easy to know, and strictly applied.

'Law is the authoritative principle for the people, and is the basis of government; it is what shapes the people. Trying to govern while eliminating the law is like a desire not to be hungry while eliminating food, or a desire not to be cold while eliminating clothes, or a desire to go east while one moves west. It is clear enough that there is no hope of realising it.

'That a hundred men will chase after a single hare that runs away, is not for the sake of the hare; for when they are sold everywhere on the market, even a thief does not dare to take one away, because their legal title is definite. Thus if the legal title is not definite, then even men like Yao, Shun, Yü or T'ang would all rush to chase after it, but if the legal title is definite even a poor thief would not take it. Now if laws and mandates are not clear, nor their titles definite, the men of the empire have opportunities for discussion; in their discussions they will differ, and there will be no definiteness. If, above, the ruler of men makes laws, but below the inferior people discuss them, the laws will not be definite and inferiors will become superiors. This may be called a condition where rights and duties are indefinite. When rights and duties are indefinite, even men like Yao and Shun will become crooked and commit acts of wickedness. How much more then the mass of the people! This is the way in which wickedness and wrongdoing will be greatly stimulated, the ruler of men will be despoiled of his authority and power, will ruin his country and bring disaster upon the altar of the soil and grain.[4]

'Now the former sages made writings and transmitted them to later generations, and it is necessary to accept these as authoritative, so that one may know what is conveyed by established terminology.[5] Should they not be accepted as authoritative, and should people discuss them according to ideas of their own mind, then until their death they will not succeed in understanding the terminology and its meaning. Therefore did the sages set up officers and officials for the laws and mandates, who should be authoritative in the empire, in order to define everyone's rights and duties, so that these being definite, the very crafty would become faithful and trustworthy, and the people would all become honest and guileless, each one restraining himself. For indeed, the defining of everybody's rights and duties is the road that leads to orderly government, but the not defining of everybody's rights and duties is the road that leads to disorder. So where there is a tendency towards order, there cannot be disorder, and where there is a tendency towards disorder, there cannot be order. Indeed, where there is a tendency towards disorder and one governs it, the disorder will only increase, but where there is a tendency towards order and one governs it, there will be order. Therefore, the sage kings governed order and did not govern disorder.

'Indeed, subtle and mysterious words which have to be pondered over cause difficulty even to men of superior knowledge. There may be one case in ten millions where the directing guidance of the law is not needed, and yet it is correct in everything. Therefore a sage governs the empire for the ten

4 i.e. his dynasty.
5 'terminology', i.e. the definition of all ethical, social and legal values, rights, duties and punishments.

million cases. For indeed, one should not make laws so that only the intelligent can understand them, for the people are not all intelligent; and one should not make laws so that only the men of talent can understand them, for the people are not all talented. Therefore did the sages, in creating laws, make them clear and easy to understand, and the terminology correct, so that stupid and wise without exception could understand them; and by setting up law officers, and officers presiding over the law, to be authoritative in the empire, prevented the people from falling into dangerous pitfalls. So the fact that when the sages established the empire there were no victims of capital punishment, was not because capital punishment did not exist, but because the laws which were applied were clear and easy to understand. They set up law officers and government officials to be the authority, in order to guide them; and they knew that if the ten thousands of people all knew what to avoid and what to strive for, they would avoid misfortune and strive for happiness, and so restrain themselves. Therefore, an intelligent prince follows the existing conditions of order and so makes the order complete, with the result that the empire will enjoy great order.'

27

(Lost)

28

(Lost)

29

(Lost)

WORDSWORTH CLASSICS OF WORLD LITERATURE